Betty Crocker's
COOKY BOOK

Illustrations by Eric Mulvany

Twenty-first Printing, 1977

Copyright © 1977, 1963 by General Mills, Inc., Minneapolis, Minn. All rights reserved.
No portion of this book may be reprinted in any form without the written
permission of the publishers, except by a reviewer who wishes to quote brief
passages in connection with a review. Produced in the U.S.A.

Library of Congress Catalog Card Number: 63–14912

Golden and Golden Press ® are trademarks of Western Publishing Company, Inc.

GOLDEN PRESS · NEW YORK
Western Publishing Company, Inc.
Racine, Wisconsin

Dear Friend,

There is no aroma quite so inviting as that of cookies baking, whether ginger or chocolate or caramel. And there is no snack quite so satisfying as two or three fresh-from-the oven cookies with a cool glass of milk Nor is there a gift quite so welcome as a lovingly wrapped package from home, brimming with cookies.

In this book you'll find cookies in variety, cherished recipes from the past and recipes using the newest convenience products, hearty fruit-filled cookies and dainty decorated ones. First come the basic how-to's of cooky-making called the Cooky Primer. Holiday cookies are next, with dozens of Christmas specialties to give and to serve. The Family Favorites chapter is chock full of cookies for lunchtime, snacktime, anytime —— such good eating that we call them disappearing cookies. For treats on short notice, turn to Quick'n Easy Cookies, featuring variations of handy baking mixes. Following are Company-Best Cookies for teatime, some of them from far-off lands. The Best Cookies from my Kitchens down through the years complete the book.

Remembering the motto "happy the home with the full cooky jar", we hope you'll turn to this book often.

Cordially,

Betty Crocker

Table of Contents

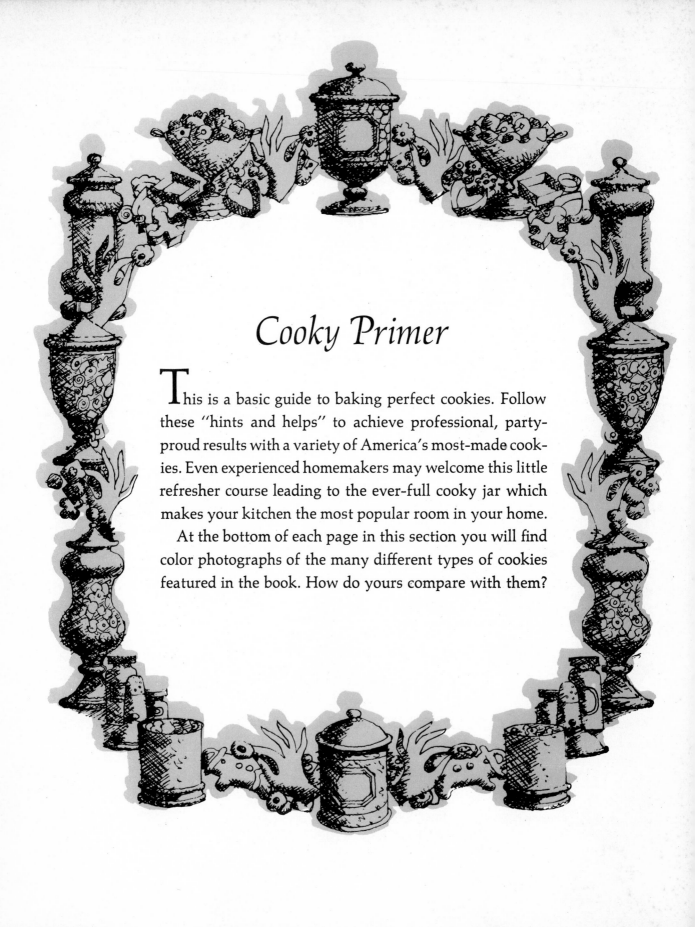

Cooky Primer

This is a basic guide to baking perfect cookies. Follow these "hints and helps" to achieve professional, party-proud results with a variety of America's most-made cookies. Even experienced homemakers may welcome this little refresher course leading to the ever-full cooky jar which makes your kitchen the most popular room in your home.

At the bottom of each page in this section you will find color photographs of the many different types of cookies featured in the book. How do yours compare with them?

Necessary Utensils

Measuring spoons

Graduated measuring cups

Liquid measuring cups

Mixing bowls

Wooden spoon

Rotary egg beater or
electric mixer

Baking sheets and pans. (Use
baking sheets or pans at least
2″ narrower and shorter
than oven so heat will
circulate around them. Shiny,
bright sheets and pans are
best for delicate browning.)

Spatula . . . for removing cookies
from baking sheet to
cooling rack

Timer

Cooling racks . . . to prevent
soggy cookies

How to Measure Flour by Dipping

*Use this easy time-saving method or the traditional
sifting method, whichever you prefer.*

1 Dip graduated measuring cups
into flour sack or canister.

2 Level off with spatula or straight-
edged knife. Do not tap cup or
pack more flour into cup before
leveling off.

3 Pour flour into mixing bowl with
other ingredients. Or stir flour and
other dry ingredients together.

Baking Hints

1 Use unsalted fat for greasing baking sheets and
pans. Check recipe, as some rich cookies need not be
baked on greased sheets.

2 Try to make all cookies in a batch the same size
to insure uniform baking.

3 Bake a test cooky to see if consistency of dough
is right. If cooky spreads more than desired, add 1 to
2 more tbsp. flour. If cooky seems dry or crumbly,
add 1 to 2 tbsp. cream to dough.

4 If baking one sheet of cookies at a time, bake in
center of oven. If baking two sheets, place oven racks
so oven is divided in thirds.

5 Look at cookies when minimum baking time is up.
Try not to overbake. Remove from baking sheet to
cooling rack with spatula immediately because cookies
continue to bake until removed from baking sheet.

6 If possible, have a second cool baking sheet ready
as cooky dough spreads on a hot baking sheet.

How to Store Cookies

Store crisp, thin cookies in container with loose cover.
Store soft cookies in container with a tight-fitting
cover.

How to Freeze Cookies

Baked cookies and cooky dough may be stored frozen 9 to 12 months. Pack baked cookies in a rigid
box, lining the box and separating each layer of
cookies with transparent plastic wrap. The clinging
quality of the plastic keeps air from reaching and drying out the cookies. Shape refrigerator cooky dough
in roll; wrap in foil or transparent plastic wrap. Place
drop or rolled cooky dough in frozen food container
or wrap in foil or transparent plastic wrap.

Can Self-Rising Flour Be Used for Cookies?

Yes, self-rising flour can be used for baking cookies.
Though usually used for quick breads, it can also be
used for other bakings. However, since leavening and
salt are already in the flour, special adjustments need
to be made. Directions for these adjustments appear
in a note below each recipe for a cooky made with
flour in this book.

What Causes Dry Cooky Dough?

There are a number of possible causes. Study the list below, then reread your recipe and you should be able to find the cause.

1 Overmeasurement of flour or dryness of flour. The properties which make flour a "structure builder" in baking also make it absorb and release moisture from the air very readily. Flour stored in a warm, dry kitchen absorbs more moisture (water, milk, or egg) than flour stored in a humid kitchen; thus, it makes a drier dough.

2 Undermeasurement of shortening or use of chilled shortening. If shortening (butter, margarine, or soft shortening) is firm, dough will be less pliable than if shortening is at room temperature.

3 Undermeasurement of liquid or use of small eggs. In some cooky recipes, eggs are the only source of moisture.

How Can Dry Cooky Dough Be Corrected?

Work 1 or 2 tbsp. soft butter or cream into dough with your hands.

How Can Dry Cooky Dough Be Prevented?

1 Measure all ingredients carefully and accurately, using standard measuring cups and spoons.

2 Have shortening at room temperature. However, shortening should not be melted.

What Causes Soft Cooky Dough?

A variety of factors may cause soft doughs which are too soft to roll or spread when baked. They are:

1 Undermeasurement of flour or use of flour that has been stored when humidity was high.

2 Overmeasurement of shortening, butter, or margarine or use of extremely soft or melted shortening.

3 Overmeasurement of liquid or use of extremely large eggs.

4 Dough mixed in a very warm room.

How Can Soft Cooky Dough Be Corrected?

Chill dough until firm enough to handle; then work with it in small portions, leaving rest of dough in refrigerator until needed. If dough is still soft after chilling, work in more flour, one tablespoon at a time; then bake a test cooky.

How Can Soft Cooky Dough Be Prevented?

1 Measure each ingredient accurately and follow mixing directions exactly.

2 Use soft butter, shortening, or margarine; do not use melted shortening.

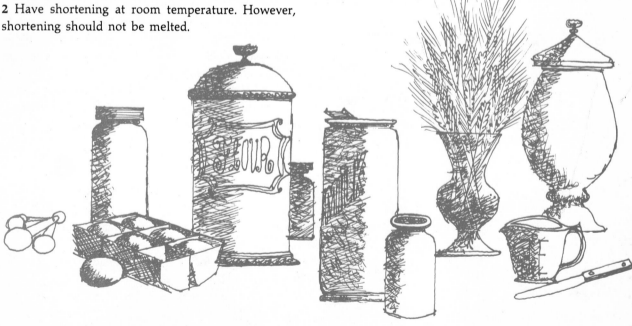

How to Make Perfect Drop Cookies

Mix dough as directed. If dough is soft, chill. Spoon up dough as recipe directs. Push dough onto baking sheet with another spoon, peaking up dough.

Bake minimum time in preheated oven. Test cookies by touching center lightly with finger. If almost no imprint remains and cooky is golden brown, it is done.

Perfect drop cookies have:
- *fairly uniform mound shape*
- *delicately browned exterior*
- *good flavor*

APPLESAUCE COOKIES

1 cup shortening
2 cups brown sugar (packed)
2 eggs
½ cup cold coffee
2 cups well-drained thick applesauce
3½ cups all-purpose flour

1 tsp. soda
1 tsp. salt
1 tsp. each cinnamon, nutmeg, and cloves
1 cup raisins
½ cup coarsely chopped nuts

Mix shortening, sugar, and eggs thoroughly. Stir in coffee and applesauce. Measure flour by dipping method (p. 5) or by sifting. Mix remaining ingredients; stir into applesauce mixture. Chill at least 2 hr.

Heat oven to 400° (mod. hot). Drop rounded tablespoonfuls of dough about 2″ apart on lightly greased baking sheet. Bake 9 to 12 min., or until almost no imprint remains when touched lightly. If desired, frost when cool with Lemon Butter Icing (p. 150). *Makes 7 to 8 doz. cookies.*

Note: *If you use self-rising flour, omit soda and salt.*

ORANGE DROP COOKIES

The recipe for this delightful cake-like cooky came to us from Mrs. Paul Lindemeyer, Mason City, Iowa. For variety, add ½ cup chopped nuts or ½ cup raisins to the dough. See color picture, pp. 86-87.

⅔ cup shortening
¾ cup sugar
1 egg
½ cup orange juice
2 tbsp. grated orange rind

2 cups all-purpose flour
½ tsp. baking powder
½ tsp. soda
½ tsp. salt
Orange Butter Icing (p. 150)

Heat oven to 400° (mod. hot). Mix shortening, sugar, and egg thoroughly. Stir in orange juice and rind. Measure flour by dipping method (p. 5) or by sifting. Stir dry ingredients together; blend in. Drop rounded teaspoonfuls of dough about 2″ apart on ungreased baking sheet. Bake 8 to 10 min., or until delicately browned on edges. Frost with Icing. *Makes 4 doz. 2″ cookies.*

Note: *If you use self-rising flour, omit baking powder, soda, and salt.*

Chocolate Chip Cookies (p. 144)

Holiday Fruit Drops (p. 146)

Kisses (p. 121)

CHOCOLATE DROP COOKIES

½ cup butter or
   margarine,
   softened
1 cup sugar
1 egg
2 sq. unsweetened
   chocolate (2 oz.),
   melted and cooled

⅓ cup buttermilk
1 tsp. vanilla
1¾ cups all-purpose
   flour
½ tsp. soda
½ tsp. salt
1 cup chopped nuts,
   if desired

Mix butter, sugar, egg, and chocolate thoroughly. Stir in buttermilk and vanilla. Measure flour by dipping method (p. 5) or by sifting. Stir together flour, soda, and salt; blend in. Mix in nuts. Chill at least 1 hr.

Heat oven to 400° (mod. hot). Drop rounded teaspoonfuls of dough about 2″ apart on ungreased baking sheet. Bake 8 to 10 min., or until no imprint remains when touched lightly. If desired, frost cooled cookies with Browned Butter Glaze (p. 151), Mocha Butter Icing (p. 150), or Marie's Chocolate Icing (p. 150) and sprinkle with chopped nuts or flaked coconut. *Makes 4½ doz. 2½″ cookies.*

Note: *If you use self-rising flour, omit soda and salt.*

COCOA DROP COOKIES

Make Chocolate Drop Cookies (above)—except increase butter to ⅔ cup; omit chocolate and add ½ cup cocoa to dry ingredients.

CHOCOLATE CHERRY DROPS

Make Chocolate Drop Cookies (above)—except omit nuts and add 2 cups cut-up candied or drained maraschino cherries.

DOUBLE CHOCOLATE DROPS

Make Chocolate Drop Cookies (above)—except add 1 cup (6-oz. pkg.) semi-sweet chocolate pieces.

BROWN SUGAR DROPS

One of the most versatile cooky doughs ever tested. Try these variations, then work out some of your own. A soft, chewy cooky with the refreshing flavor of brown sugar.

1 cup shortening
2 cups brown sugar
   (packed)
2 eggs
½ cup buttermilk
   or water

3½ cups all-purpose
   flour
1 tsp. soda
1 tsp. salt

Mix shortening, sugar, and eggs thoroughly. Stir in buttermilk. Measure flour by dipping method (p. 5) or by sifting. Stir flour, soda, and salt together; blend into sugar mixture. Chill at least 1 hr.

Heat oven to 400° (mod. hot). Drop rounded teaspoonfuls of dough about 2″ apart on lightly greased baking sheet. Bake 8 to 10 min., or until almost no imprint remains when touched lightly. *Makes about 6 doz. 2½″ cookies.*

Note: *If you use self-rising flour, omit soda and salt.*

JEWELED COOKIES

Make Brown Sugar Drops (above)—except mix 3 to 4 cups cut-up gumdrops into the dough. (It's easy to cut up gumdrops using kitchen shears. If blades get sticky, dip them in warm water.)

NUT DROP COOKIES

Make Brown Sugar Drops (above)—except mix 1 cup chopped nuts into the dough.

COCONUT DROP COOKIES

Make Brown Sugar Drops (above)—except mix 1 cup moist shredded or flaked coconut into the dough.

Chocolate Drop
Cookies (above)

Chocolate Cherry Drops (above)

Coconut-Cherry Cookies (p. 70)

Satin-glazed Date Drops (p. 40)

PINEAPPLE COOKIES

1 cup shortening
1½ cups sugar
1 egg
1 can (8¼ oz.) crushed
    pineapple, with
    juice

3½ cups all-purpose
    flour
1 tsp. soda
½ tsp. salt
¼ tsp. nutmeg
½ cup chopped nuts

Mix shortening, sugar, and egg thoroughly. Stir in pineapple. Measure flour by dipping method (p. 5) or by sifting. Stir together flour, soda, salt, and nutmeg; blend in. Mix in nuts. Chill at least 1 hr.

Heat oven to 400° (mod. hot). Drop rounded teaspoonfuls of dough about 2″ apart on lightly greased baking sheet. Bake 8 to 10 min., or until no imprint remains when touched lightly. *Makes about 5 doz. cookies.*

Note: *If you use self-rising flour, omit soda and salt.*

PINEAPPLE COCONUT COOKIES

Make Pineapple Cookies (above)—except omit nutmeg and add 1 cup flaked coconut.

PINEAPPLE RAISIN COOKIES

Make Pineapple Cookies (above)—except add 1 cup raisins.

OLD-FASHIONED OATMEAL COOKIES

Soft and moist on the inside and crisp on the outside. See color picture, pp. 86-87.

1 cup raisins
1 cup water
¾ cup shortening
1½ cups sugar
2 eggs
1 tsp. vanilla
2½ cups all-purpose
    flour

½ tsp. baking powder
1 tsp. soda
1 tsp. salt
1 tsp. cinnamon
½ tsp. cloves
2 cups rolled oats
½ cup chopped nuts

Simmer raisins and water in saucepan over low heat until raisins are plump, 20 to 30 min. Drain raisin liquid into measuring cup. Add enough water to make ½ cup.

Heat oven to 400° (mod. hot). Mix shortening, sugar, eggs, and vanilla. Stir in raisin liquid. Measure flour by dipping method (p. 5) or by sifting. Stir together flour, baking powder, soda, salt, and spices; blend in. Add rolled oats, nuts, and raisins. Drop rounded teaspoonfuls of dough about 2″ apart on ungreased baking sheet. Bake 8 to 10 min., or until lightly browned. *Makes 6 to 7 doz. cookies.*

Note: *If you use self-rising flour, omit baking powder, soda, and salt.*

Pineapple Raisin Cookies (above)   Pineapple Coconut Cookies (above)   Salted Peanut Crisps (p. 147)

MOLASSES JUMBLES

From the butter- and sugar-saving days of World War II. The recipe card carried these lines: "They're easy on the budget . . . their molasses flavor's grand. These soft delicious cookies are best in all the land." Your family will think so, too.

¼ cup plus 1 tbsp. shortening	3½ cups all-purpose flour
½ cup brown sugar (packed)	1 tbsp. soda
1 cup molasses	½ tsp. salt
	½ cup cold water

Heat oven to 375° (quick mod.). Cream shortening and sugar thoroughly. Stir in molasses. Measure flour by dipping method (p. 5) or by sifting. Stir dry ingredients together. (Don't be alarmed at amount of baking soda; it makes the cooky more tender.) Blend into creamed mixture alternately with water. Drop heaping teaspoonfuls of dough 2 to 3" apart on lightly greased baking sheet. Bake 10 to 12 min. *Makes about 4 doz. cookies.*

Note: *If you use self-rising flour, omit soda and salt.*

SPICED MOLASSES JUMBLES

Make Molasses Jumbles (above)—except blend ½ tsp. each ginger, cloves, nutmeg, and cinnamon with the dry ingredients.

LEMON MOLASSES JUMBLES

Make Molasses Jumbles (above)—except stir in grated rind of 1 lemon (about 1 tbsp.) with molasses.

FROSTED MOLASSES JUMBLES

Bake Molasses Jumbles (above). Spread tops while slightly warm with Butter Icing (p. 150).

JUBILEE JUMBLES

½ cup shortening	1 tsp. vanilla
1½ cups brown sugar (packed)	2¾ cups all-purpose flour
2 eggs	½ tsp. soda
1 cup commercial sour cream	1 tsp. salt
	1 cup chopped nuts

Mix shortening, sugar, and eggs thoroughly. Stir in sour cream and vanilla. Measure flour by dipping method (p. 5) or by sifting. Stir together flour, soda, and salt; blend in. Mix in nuts. Chill dough if soft.

Heat oven to 375° (quick mod.). Drop rounded tablespoonfuls of dough about 2" apart on greased baking sheet. Bake about 10 min., or until almost no imprint remains when touched lightly. If desired, spread cooled cookies with a double recipe of Browned Butter Glaze (p. 151). *Makes about 4 doz. 2½" cookies.*

Note: *If you use self-rising flour, omit soda and salt.*

COCONUT JUMBLES

Make Jubilee Jumbles (above)—except mix 1 cup moist flaked coconut into the dough.

DATE OR RAISIN JUMBLES

Make Jubilee Jumbles (above)—except mix 1 cup finely cut dates or raisins into the dough.

FRUIT JUMBLES

Make Jubilee Jumbles (above)—except omit nuts. Mix 2 cups candied cherries, cut into halves, 2 cups chopped dates, and 1½ cups chopped pecans into the dough. Drop rounded teaspoonfuls of dough on baking sheet. Place a pecan half on each cooky. Do not frost. *Makes about 7 doz. cookies.*

Molasses Jumbles (above)   Cranberry Drops (p. 40)   Indian Jumanas (p. 88)

How to Make Perfect Bar Cookies

Mix bar cooky dough as recipe directs. With spatula, spread dough evenly in greased square or oblong pan. Bake minimum time in preheated oven.

To test for doneness: bake fudgy-type bars until top has dull crust; bake cake-like bars until tooth-pick stuck in center comes out clean; bake meringue-topped bars until delicately browned.

Perfect bar cookies have:
- *uniform well-cut shape*
- *rich, moist eating quality*
- *thin delicate crust*
- *appealing flavor*

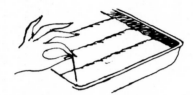

BUTTERSCOTCH BROWNIES

These rich, chewy bars keep soft and delicious for days in a tightly covered jar.

¼ cup butter, margarine, shortening, or vegetable oil	¾ cup all-purpose flour
1 cup light brown sugar (packed)	1 tsp. baking powder
1 egg	½ tsp. salt
	½ tsp. vanilla
	½ cup coarsely chopped walnuts

Heat oven to 350° (mod.). If using butter, margarine, or shortening, melt over low heat. Remove from heat; stir in sugar until blended; cool. If using oil, just blend oil and sugar. Stir in egg. Measure flour by dipping method (p. 5) or by sifting. Stir flour, baking powder, and salt together; blend in. Mix in vanilla and walnuts. Spread in well-greased square pan, 8x8x2". Bake 25 min. Do not overbake! Cut in bars while warm. *Makes 18 bars about 2½x1".*

Note: *If you use self-rising flour, omit salt; reduce baking powder to ½ tsp.*

BUTTERSCOTCH COCONUT BROWNIES

Make Butterscotch Brownies (left)—except use ½ cup finely chopped coconut instead of nuts.

BUTTERSCOTCH DATE BROWNIES

Make Butterscotch Brownies (left)—except add ½ cup finely cut dates.

BUTTERSCOTCH CUT-OUTS

Make Butterscotch Brownies (left)—except use only ¼ cup finely chopped nuts. Spread in greased oblong pan, 13x9½x2". Bake 15 min., being careful not to overbake. While still warm, cut in fancy shapes with cooky cutters.

BRAZIL NUT BUTTERSCOTCH BROWNIES

Make Butterscotch Brownies (left)—except use ¾ cup ground Brazil nuts in place of walnuts.

Butterscotch Brownies
(above)

Angel Sandwiches
(p. 113)

Date-Nut Squares
(p. 68)

DATE BARS

Date Filling (below)	1¾ cups all-purpose
¾ cup shortening	flour
(part butter or	½ tsp. soda
margarine)	1 tsp. salt
1 cup brown sugar	1½ cups rolled oats
(packed)	

Prepare Date Filling; let cool. Heat oven to 400° (mod. hot). Mix shortening and sugar thoroughly. Stir flour, soda, and salt together; blend in. Mix in rolled oats. Press and flatten half of mixture over bottom of greased oblong pan, 13x9½x2″. Spread with cooled Filling. Top with remaining crumb mixture, patting lightly. Bake 25 to 30 min., or until lightly browned. While warm, cut in bars and remove from pan. *Makes about 2½ doz. 2x1½″ bars.*

Note: *If you use self-rising flour, omit soda and salt.*

Date Filling: Mix 3 cups cut-up dates, ¼ cup sugar, and 1½ cups water in saucepan. Cook over low heat, stirring constantly, until thickened (about 10 min.). Cool before using.

DATE-APRICOT BARS

Make Date Bars (left)—except use Date-Apricot Filling (below).

Date-Apricot Filling: Mix 1 cup cut-up dates, 2 cups mashed cooked dried apricots (drained), ½ cup sugar, and 2 tbsp. apricot juice in saucepan. Cook over low heat, stirring constantly, until thickened (about 5 min.). Cool before using.

PINEAPPLE BARS

Make Date Bars (left)—except use Pineapple Filling (below).

Pineapple Filling: Mix 1 cup crushed pineapple and juice (8¼-oz. can), 1 cup sugar, 2½ tbsp. cornstarch, 1 tbsp. butter, and 1 cup water in saucepan. Cook until thickened; cool.

JAM BARS

Make Date Bars (left)—except use 1 cup jam in place of Date Filling; strawberry jam or cherry-pineapple preserves are especially good.

LEMONADE PRUNE BARS

Make Date Bars (left)—except use Lemonade Prune Filling (below).

Lemonade Prune Filling: Simmer 2 cups very finely cut-up uncooked prunes in 1 can (6 oz.) frozen lemonade and 1 lemonade can of water in covered saucepan until soft, about 15 min. Blend in ⅔ cup sugar, ¼ cup all-purpose flour, and ¼ tsp. salt. Add ½ cup chopped nuts. Cool.

Plantation
Fruit Bars (p. 79)

Toffee Squares
(p. 39)

White Fruit Bars
(p. 41)

TEEN-TIME CHOCOLATE NUT BARS

1 cup brown sugar (packed)	1 tsp. baking powder
½ cup butter or margarine	¼ tsp. soda
½ cup milk	2 eggs
1¼ cups all-purpose flour	1 cup (6-oz. pkg.) semi-sweet chocolate pieces
1 tsp. salt	1 cup coarsely chopped nuts

Heat oven to 350° (mod.). Blend sugar, butter, and milk in saucepan. Bring just to a boil, stirring constantly. Cool 5 min. Measure flour by dipping method (p. 5) or by sifting. Blend flour, salt, baking powder, and soda. Beat eggs into butter mixture. Add flour mixture; mix thoroughly. Stir in chocolate pieces and nuts. Spread in greased and floured oblong pan, 13x9½x2". Bake 25 min. Cool; cut in 2x1" bars. *Makes about 4 doz. bars.*

Note: *If you use self-rising flour, omit salt, baking powder, and soda.*

LEMON SQUARES

1 cup all-purpose flour	2 eggs
½ cup butter or margarine	1 cup granulated sugar
¼ cup confectioners' sugar	½ tsp. baking powder
	¼ tsp. salt
	2 tbsp. lemon juice

Heat oven to 350° (mod.). Measure flour by dipping method (p. 5) or by sifting. Blend flour, butter, and confectioners' sugar thoroughly. Press evenly in square pan, 8x8x2", building up ½" edge. Bake 20 min. Beat rest of ingredients together. Pour over crust and bake about 25 min. more or just until no imprint remains when touched lightly in center. *Makes 25 squares.*

Note: *If you use self-rising flour, omit baking powder and salt.*

DREAM BARS

½ cup shortening (part butter or margarine)	1 cup all-purpose flour
½ cup brown sugar (packed)	Almond-Coconut Topping (below)

Heat oven to 350° (mod.). Mix shortening and sugar thoroughly. Stir in flour. Press and flatten with hand to cover bottom of ungreased oblong pan, 13x9½x2". Bake 10 min. Then spread with Topping. Return to oven and bake 25 min. more, or until golden brown. Cool slightly, then cut in bars. *Makes about 2½ doz. 3x1" bars.*

Almond-Coconut Topping

2 eggs, well beaten	½ tsp. salt
1 cup brown sugar (packed)	1 cup moist shredded coconut
1 tsp. vanilla	1 cup slivered almonds (or other nuts)
2 tbsp. flour	
1 tsp. baking powder	

Mix eggs, sugar, and vanilla. Mix with flour, baking powder, and salt. Stir in coconut and almonds.

Note: *If you use self-rising flour, omit baking powder and salt from topping.*

CHOCOLATE CHIP DREAM BARS

Make Dream Bars (above)—except use ⅓ cup butter or margarine in bottom layer. In topping, use 1 pkg. (6 oz.) semi-sweet chocolate pieces in place of coconut. Bake 15 to 20 min. Cool; spread with Thin Chocolate Icing (p. 151).

Cherry-Coconut Bars
(p. 41)

Lemon Squares
(above)

Dream Bars (above)

CHOCOLATE FRUIT BARS

Delightful for entertaining or as family fare.

1¼ cups all-purpose
  flour
1½ tsp. baking powder
1 tsp. salt
3 eggs
1 cup sugar
½ tsp. almond extract
1 pkg. (6 oz.) semi-
  sweet chocolate
  pieces

1 cup chopped dates
  or raisins
½ cup chopped
  maraschino
  cherries, drained
1 cup chopped
  walnuts

Heat oven to 350° (mod.). Measure flour by dipping method (p. 5) or by sifting. Stir flour, baking powder, and salt together. Beat eggs until light; add sugar gradually, beating well after each addition. Stir in almond flavoring, then dry ingredients. Fold in chocolate pieces, fruits, and nuts. Spread dough evenly in greased oblong pan, 13x9½x2". Bake 30 to 35 min. If desired, when cool, frost with confectioners' sugar icing. Cut in bars; garnish each bar with a chocolate piece. *Makes 3 doz. bars.*

Note: *If you use self-rising flour, omit baking powder and salt.*

COCONUT APRICOT STRIPS

Serve tiny bars the same day they are made.

½ cup shortening
  (half butter or
  margarine)
½ cup confectioners'
  sugar
2 egg yolks
1 cup all-purpose
  flour

½ cup thick apricot
  preserves
½ cup thick
  pineapple
  preserves
Coconut Meringue
  (below)

Heat oven to 350° (mod.). Mix shortening, sugar, and egg yolks thoroughly. Measure flour by dipping method (p. 5) or by sifting. Stir flour into sugar mixture. Press and flatten mixture to cover bottom of ungreased oblong pan, 13x9½x2". Bake 10 min. Remove from oven and spread with preserves, then with Meringue. Return to oven; bake about 20 min., until Meringue is golden brown. Cool slightly; cut in small bars, about 2x1". *Makes about 4 doz. bars.*

Note: *If desired, self-rising flour may be used.*

Coconut Meringue: Beat 2 egg whites until frothy. Gradually add ½ cup sugar; beat until stiff and glossy. Fold in ½ cup flaked coconut.

Chocolate Fruit Bars
(above)

Coconut-Chocolate
Meringue Bites
(p. 116)

Coconut Apricot
Strips (above)

How to Make Perfect Refrigerator Cookies

Mix dough as directed. With hands, shape dough into long, smooth roll of diameter recipe suggests. If desired, add a festive touch by rolling in finely chopped nuts, colored sugar, or chocolate shot.

Wrap in waxed paper, twisting ends. Chill in refrigerator until firm enough to slice easily. When ready to bake, slice desired thickness using thin, sharp knife. You can refrigerate 3 to 4 days.

Perfect refrigerator cookies have:
- *uniform, thin slices*
- *lightly browned surface*
- *crisp, crunchy texture*
- *rich flavor*

CHOCOLATE REFRIGERATOR COOKIES

Rich and buttery. See color picture, pp. 114–115.

1¼ cups butter or margarine	½ cup cocoa
1½ cups sifted confectioners' sugar	¼ tsp. salt
	1½ cups chopped pecans
1 egg	4 oz. sweet cooking chocolate
3 cups cake flour	

Cream butter and sugar. Blend in egg. Measure flour by spooning into cup and leveling off or by sifting. Stir flour, cocoa, and salt into butter mixture; blend well. Chill dough 1 to 2 hr. Press and mold into 2 long, smooth rolls, each about 1½" in diameter. Roll in pecans pressing them in on all sides. Chill overnight.

Heat oven to 400° (mod. hot). Cut in ⅛" slices. Place on ungreased baking sheet. Bake about 10 min. Cool. Melt chocolate in double boiler; frost center of cookies. *Makes about 8 doz. cookies.*

GINGER ALMOND COOKIES

Flecks of white almond in the dark ginger-molasses dough make this a most attractive cooky. A taste delight for everyone.

1½ cups shortening	1½ tsp. salt
1½ cups sugar	1 tbsp. plus 1 tsp. ginger
¾ cup light molasses	1 tbsp. cinnamon
4 cups all-purpose flour	1 tbsp. cloves
1½ tsp. soda	1½ cups almonds, finely chopped

Cream shortening, sugar, and molasses until fluffy. Measure flour by dipping method (p. 5) or by sifting. Mix dry ingredients; stir into creamed mixture. Add almonds. Shape in 2 thick rolls, each 2" in diameter. Wrap in waxed paper; refrigerate several hours until very firm.

Heat oven to 350° (mod.). Cut in ¼" slices. Bake on lightly greased baking sheet 12 to 15 min. *Makes about 7½ doz. cookies.*

Note: *If you use self-rising flour, omit soda and salt.*

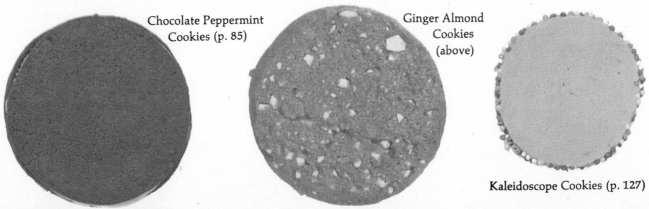

Chocolate Peppermint Cookies (p. 85)

Ginger Almond Cookies (above)

Kaleidoscope Cookies (p. 127)

VANILLA REFRIGERATOR COOKIES

1 cup shortening	1½ tsp. vanilla
½ cup granulated sugar	2¾ cups all-purpose flour
½ cup brown sugar (packed)	½ tsp. soda
2 eggs	1 tsp. salt

Mix shortening, sugars, eggs, and vanilla thoroughly. Measure flour by dipping method (p. 5) or by sifting. Blend dry ingredients together; mix into shortening mixture. Mix thoroughly with hands. Press and mold into a long, smooth roll about 2½″ in diameter. Wrap in waxed paper; chill several hours or overnight.

Heat oven to 400° (mod. hot). Cut in thin slices (⅛ to 1/16″ thick). Place a little apart on ungreased baking sheet. Bake 6 to 8 min., or until lightly browned. *Makes about 6 doz. 2½″ cookies.*

Note: *If you use self-rising flour, omit salt; reduce soda to ¼ tsp.*

NUT REFRIGERATOR COOKIES

Make Vanilla Refrigerator Cookies (above)—except mix ½ cup cut-up nuts into dough.

CINNAMON SLICES

Make Vanilla Refrigerator Cookies (above)—except use 2 to 3 tsp. cinnamon in place of vanilla.

DATE-NUT REFRIGERATOR COOKIES

Make Vanilla Refrigerator Cookies (above)—except mix ½ cup finely cut dates and ½ cup finely chopped nuts into dough.

CHOCOLATE SLICES

Make Vanilla Refrigerator Cookies (above)—except blend 2 sq. unsweetened chocolate (2 oz.), melted and cooled, into shortening mixture.

OATMEAL COCONUT CRISPIES

1 cup shortening (part butter or margarine)	1 tsp. vanilla
	2½ cups all-purpose flour
1 cup granulated sugar	1 tsp. soda
1 cup brown sugar (packed)	1 tsp. salt
	1 cup rolled oats
2 eggs	1 cup flaked coconut

Mix shortening, sugars, eggs, and vanilla until fluffy. Measure flour by dipping method (p. 5) or by sifting. Blend flour, soda, and salt thoroughly; stir into shortening mixture. Blend in rolled oats and coconut. (Dough will be soft.) Shape in 2 rolls, each about 2″ in diameter. Wrap in waxed paper; refrigerate overnight.

Heat oven to 400° (mod. hot). Cut in ¼″ slices. Place on lightly greased baking sheet. Bake 10 to 12 min., or until lightly browned. *Makes about 7 doz. cookies.*

Note: *If you use self-rising flour, omit soda and salt.*

OATMEAL COCONUT DROPS

Make Oatmeal Coconut Crispies (above)—except use only 1¾ cups all-purpose flour; drop dough by rounded teaspoonfuls on lightly greased baking sheet.

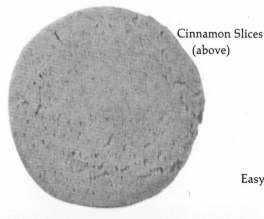

Cinnamon Slices (above)

Easy Chinese Almond Cookies (p. 89)

Oatmeal Coconut Crispies (above)

DATE-NUT PINWHEELS

Make dough for Caramel Refrigerator Cookies (p. 145). Divide in half. Roll each piece of dough on waxed paper into rectangle about 11x7". Spread rectangles with Date-Nut Filling (below). Roll up tightly, beginning at wide side. Pinch edge to seal. Wrap each roll in waxed paper and chill several hours.

Heat oven to 400° (mod. hot). Cut in ¼" slices. Place on lightly greased baking sheet. Bake about 10 min., or until lightly browned. *Makes about 5 doz. cookies.*

Date-Nut Filling: Cook ¾ lb. moist pitted dates, cut-up; ⅓ cup sugar; ⅓ cup water in saucepan until slightly thickened, stirring constantly. Remove from heat. Cool. Stir in ½ cup finely chopped nuts.

PEANUT BUTTER HONEY COOKIES

⅓ cup shortening (part butter or margarine)	2 cups all-purpose flour
½ cup sugar	1 tsp. baking powder
½ cup honey or corn syrup	¼ tsp. soda
⅔ cup peanut butter	½ tsp. salt
1 egg	½ cup peanuts, chopped

Mix shortening, sugar, honey, peanut butter, and egg thoroughly. Measure flour by dipping method (p. 5) or by sifting. Blend dry ingredients; stir into shortening mixture. Stir in nuts. Shape into a strip about 10x2½x1½". Wrap in waxed paper; store in refrigerator for several hours. Bake as needed.

Heat oven to 400° (mod. hot). Cut dough in ⅛" slices with a sharp knife. Place about 1" apart on greased baking sheet; bake 8 to 10 min. *Makes about 6½ doz. cookies.*

Note: *If you use self-rising flour, omit baking powder and salt.*

REFRIGERATOR FILLED COOKIES

Filling between two cooky slices makes a little mound that gives cooky an island shape.

½ cup shortening (part butter or margarine)	1 egg
	1¼ cups plus 2 tbsp. all-purpose flour
¼ cup granulated sugar	¼ tsp. soda
	½ tsp. salt
¼ cup brown sugar (packed)	Fruit or Mincemeat Filling (below)

Mix shortening, sugars, and egg thoroughly. Measure flour by dipping method (p. 5) or by sifting. Blend flour, soda, salt; stir into shortening mixture. Mix with hands. Press and mold into a long smooth roll about 1½" in diameter. Wrap in waxed paper; chill several hours or overnight.

Heat oven to 400° (mod. hot). With a thin, sharp knife, cut ⅛" thick slices. (Chill half the dough while cutting the other half.) Place a little apart on ungreased baking sheet. Put ½ tsp. Filling on each cooky. Put another cooky on top. Bake 8 to 10 min., or until lightly browned. *Makes 2½ doz. cookies.*

Note: *If you use self-rising flour, omit salt; reduce soda to ⅛ tsp.*

Fruit Filling: Cook ½ cup chopped dates, apricots, figs, or whole raisins; ¼ cup sugar; ¼ cup water together about 5 min. until thick. Remove from heat. Stir in ½ cup chopped walnuts.

Mincemeat Filling: Mix ¼ cup mincemeat, 2 tbsp. nuts, and 1 tbsp. maraschino cherries (cut in quarters).

Date Pinwheels
(above)

Half 'N Half Slices
(p. 115)

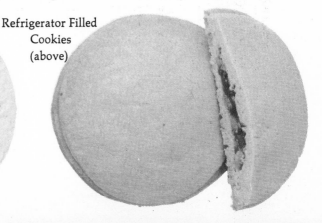

Refrigerator Filled
Cookies
(above)

How to Make Perfect Rolled Cookies

Mix dough as directed. Using part of dough and keeping rest chilled, lightly roll dough to desired thickness; the thinner you roll, the crisper the cookies. Rub flour into rolling pin cover and cloth to prevent sticking.

To cut: dip cooky cutter in flour, shake off excess, cut with steady pressure. Cut as many cookies from each rolling as possible. Cut diamonds or squares with knife. Carefully lift cut-out cookies to baking sheet with spatula. Bake.

Perfect rolled cookies have:
- *uniform shape of cutter*
- *lightly browned surface*
- *crisp texture or soft texture, depending on thickness*
- *rich, delicate flavor*

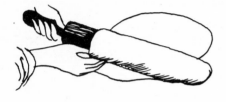

ETHEL'S SUGAR COOKIES

A time-tested family favorite . . . made with granulated sugar.

¾ cup shortening (part butter or margarine)
1 cup sugar
2 eggs
½ tsp. lemon flavoring or 1 tsp. vanilla

2½ cups all-purpose flour
1 tsp. baking powder
1 tsp. salt

Mix shortening, sugar, eggs, and flavoring thoroughly. Measure flour by dipping method (p. 5) or by sifting. Stir flour, baking powder, and salt together; blend in. Chill at least 1 hr.

Heat oven to 400° (mod. hot). Roll dough ⅛" thick on lightly floured board. Cut with 3" cooky cutter. Place on ungreased baking sheet. Bake 6 to 8 min., or until cookies are a delicate golden color. *Makes about 4 doz. cookies.*

Note: *If you use self-rising flour, omit baking powder and salt.*

MARY'S SUGAR COOKIES

From Mary Herman . . . made with confectioners' sugar.

1½ cups sifted confectioners' sugar
1 cup butter or margarine
1 egg
1 tsp. vanilla

½ tsp. almond flavoring
2½ cups all-purpose flour
1 tsp. soda
1 tsp. cream of tartar

Mix sugar and butter. Add egg and flavorings; mix thoroughly. Measure flour by dipping method (p. 5) or by sifting. Stir dry ingredients together and blend in. Refrigerate 2 to 3 hr.

Heat oven to 375° (quick mod.). Divide dough in half and roll 3/16" thick on lightly floured pastry cloth. Cut with cooky cutter; sprinkle with sugar. Place on lightly greased baking sheet. Bake 7 to 8 min., or until delicately golden. *Makes 5 doz. 2 to 2½" cookies.*

Note: *If you use self-rising flour, omit soda and cream of tartar.*

Old-fashioned Sour Cream Cookies (p. 79)

Snowflakes (p. 39)

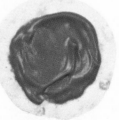

Buttery Nut Rounds (p. 52)

FILLED COOKIES

½ cup shortening	2½ cups all-purpose
1 cup sugar	flour
2 eggs	¼ tsp. soda
1 tsp. vanilla	½ tsp. salt
	Filling (right)

Mix shortening, sugar, and eggs thoroughly. Stir in vanilla. Measure flour by dipping method (p. 5) or by sifting. Stir dry ingredients together and blend in. Chill dough.

Heat oven to 400° (mod. hot). Roll dough 1/16" thick on floured board. Cut with round cutter or any desired shape about 2½" in diameter, cutting 2 alike for each filled cooky. For a decorative effect, cut the center out of the top cooky with a tiny heart, star, or scalloped cutter. Place the bottom pieces on lightly greased baking sheet. Spread a rounded teaspoonful of cooled Filling on each. Cover with top cooky. Press edges together with floured tines of fork or fingertips. Bake 8 to 10 min., or until delicately browned. *Makes 4½ doz. 2½" cookies.*

Note: *If you use self-rising flour, omit soda and salt.*

FILLED COOKY TURNOVERS

Make Filled Cookies (above)—except cut 3" rounds or squares. Place a teaspoonful of Filling on each; fold over like a turnover; press edges together. *Makes 6 doz. 3" cookies.*

Pineapple Filling

1 cup sugar	¼ cup lemon juice
¼ cup all-purpose	3 tbsp. butter
flour	¼ tsp. nutmeg
1½ cups well-drained	¾ cup pineapple
crushed pineapple	juice

Mix sugar and flour in saucepan. Stir in rest of ingredients. Cook slowly, stirring constantly, until thickened (5 to 10 min.). Cool. *Makes 2⅔ cups filling.*

Cherry Filling

1 cup sugar	24 maraschino
3 tbsp. cornstarch	cherries, chopped
1 cup orange juice	2 tbsp. butter
½ cup maraschino	
cherry juice	

Blend dry ingredients together in saucepan. Add remaining ingredients. Bring to rolling boil; boil 1 min., stirring constantly. Chill. *Makes 2⅔ cups filling.*

Date, Fig, Raisin, or Prune Filling

2 cups dates, figs, or	¾ cup sugar
raisins, finely cut	¾ cup water
up or ground, or	½ cup chopped nuts,
2 cups mashed	if desired
cooked prunes	

Cook fruit, sugar, and water together slowly, stirring constantly, until thickened. Add nuts. Cool. *Makes 2⅓ cups filling.*

HINT

Sticky fruits can be cleaned from your food grinder quickly and easily by running a few small pieces of dry bread through it.

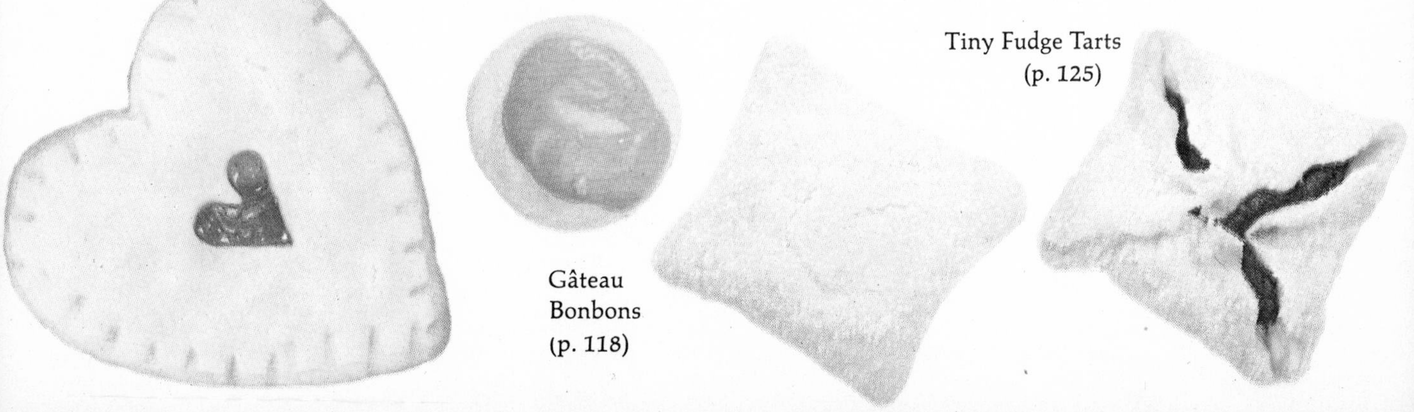

Cherry-filled Cookies (above)

Gâteau Bonbons (p. 118)

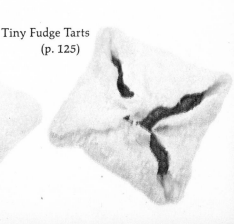

Tiny Fudge Tarts (p. 125)

MORAVIAN GINGER COOKIES

Crisp, spicy, paper-thin. The Moravians who founded Bethlehem, Pennsylvania, on Christmas Eve, 1741, brought this cooky recipe with them.

⅓ cup molasses	½ tsp. salt
¼ cup shortening	¼ tsp. soda
2 tbsp. brown sugar	¼ tsp. each cinna-
1¼ cups all-purpose	mon, ginger, and
flour	cloves
¼ tsp. baking powder	dash each nutmeg
	and allspice

Mix molasses, shortening, and sugar thoroughly. Measure flour by dipping method (p. 5) or by sifting. Stir together remaining ingredients; blend in. Work with hands until well blended. Cover; chill about 4 hr. (Thorough chilling is needed to make dough hold together.)

Heat oven to 375° (quick mod.). Roll dough out paper-thin, a little at a time. Cut in desired shapes. Place on ungreased baking sheet. Bake 8 min., or until lightly browned. If desired, frost with Easy Creamy Icing (p. 150). *Makes about 5 doz. cookies.*

Note: *If you use self-rising flour, omit baking powder, salt, and soda.*

SCOTCH SHORTBREAD

¾ cup butter	¼ cup sugar
or margarine	2 cups all-purpose
	flour

Mix butter and sugar thoroughly. Measure flour by dipping method (p. 5) or by sifting. Work in flour with hands. Chill dough.

Heat oven to 350° (mod.). Roll dough ⅓ to ½" thick. Cut into fancy shapes (small leaves, ovals, squares, etc.). Flute edges, if desired, by pinching between fingers as for pie crust. Place on ungreased baking sheet. Bake 20 to 25 min. (The tops do not brown.) *Makes about 2 doz. 1½x1" cookies.*

Note: *Do not use self-rising flour in this recipe.*

CHINESE ALMOND COOKIES

3½ cups all-purpose	1 egg, beaten
flour	2 tsp. almond extract
2 cups sugar	1 tsp. vanilla
1 tsp. baking powder	2 to 3 tbsp. whole
2 cups shortening	blanched
(part butter or	almonds
margarine)	

Heat oven to 375° (quick mod.). Measure flour by dipping method (p. 5) or by sifting. Blend flour, sugar, and baking powder. Add shortening, egg, and flavorings; mix thoroughly with hands until dough is smooth and well blended. Roll dough ¼" thick on lightly floured board; cut with 2" round cooky cutter. Put one almond in center of each cooky; place 1½" apart on ungreased baking sheet. Bake about 12 min., or until cookies are lightly browned. *Makes about 4 doz. 2" cookies.*

Note: *If you use self-rising flour, omit baking powder.*

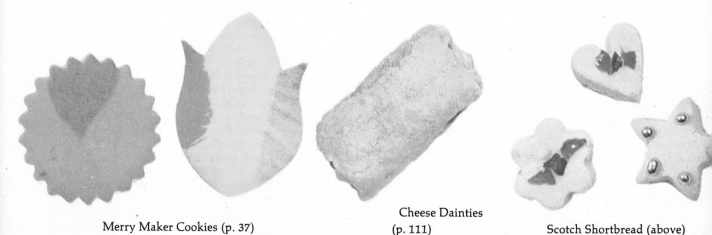

Merry Maker Cookies (p. 37)

Cheese Dainties (p. 111)

Scotch Shortbread (above)

How to Make Perfect Pressed Cookies

Mix dough as directed—doughs for pressed cookies are high in shortening. Dough must be pliable. If very warm, chill a short time. (If too cold, it crumbles.) Using ¼ at a time, place dough in cooky press.

Force dough through cooky press, following manufacturers' directions, on ungreased baking sheet. If baking sheet is too warm, fat in the dough will melt and cookies will pull away from sheet when press is lifted. Bake until set.

Perfect pressed cookies have:
- *well-defined pattern and shape*
- *tender, yet crisp eating quality*
- *rich, buttery flavor*

SPRITZ

Crisp, fragile, buttery-tasting. Use different cooky press plates for special occasions: animal shapes for children's parties, flower shapes for bridal showers, stars and trees at Christmas. See color picture, p. 36.

1 cup butter or margarine
½ cup sugar
1 egg
½ tsp. salt

1 tsp. flavoring (almond or vanilla)
2¼ cups all-purpose flour

Heat oven to 400° (mod. hot). Mix butter, sugar, egg, salt, and flavoring thoroughly. Measure flour by dipping method (p. 5) or by sifting. Work in flour. Using ¼ dough at a time, force dough through cooky press on ungreased baking sheet in desired shapes. Bake 6 to 9 min., or until set but not brown. *Makes about 5 doz. cookies.*

Note: *Do not use self-rising flour in this recipe.*

CHOCOLATE SPRITZ

See color picture, pp. 32-33.

Make Spritz (left)—except blend 2 sq. unsweetened chocolate (2 oz.), melted, into the shortening mixture.

HOLIDAY SPRITZ

Party cooky idea from Mrs. Dennis Thuftedal, Fort Worth, Texas, formerly of our staff. See color picture, pp. 32-33.

Make Spritz (left)—except omit almond or vanilla flavoring and add 1 tsp. rum flavoring. Tint dough delicate pastel shades with food coloring. If desired, glaze cooled cookies with Butter Rum Glaze (below).

Butter Rum Glaze: Melt ¼ cup butter in saucepan. Blend in 1 cup sifted confectioners' sugar and 1 tsp. rum flavoring. Stir in 1 to 2 tbsp. hot water until glaze is spreading consistency. Tint glaze to match cookies.

Holiday Spritz (above)

Spritz (above)

Chocolate Spritz (above)

PEANUT BUTTER FINGERS

Make dough for Peanut Butter Cookies (p. 24). Chill 1 hr. Heat oven to 375° (quick mod.). Using cooky press with star plate, make 2½" fingers. Bake 8 to 10 min. When cool, dip one end in melted chocolate (4 small plain chocolate bars), then in ¾ cup salted peanuts, crushed. *Makes 6 doz. cookies.*

LEMON CHEESE PRESSED COOKIES

1 cup butter or margarine	1 tbsp. lemon juice
1 pkg. (3 oz.) cream cheese	1 tsp. grated lemon rind
1 cup sugar	2½ cups all-purpose flour
1 egg, beaten	1 tsp. baking powder

Blend butter and cream cheese. Add sugar; cream thoroughly. Add egg, lemon juice, and rind; blend well. Measure flour by dipping method (p. 5) or by sifting. Blend flour and baking powder. Add to cream cheese mixture; mix thoroughly. Chill dough 30 min.

Heat oven to 375° (quick mod.). Force dough through cooky press on ungreased baking sheet. Bake 8 to 10 min., or until slightly browned. *Makes about 5 doz. 2" cookies.*

Note: *If you use self-rising flour, omit baking powder.*

CHOCOLATE PRESSED COOKIES

Make Lemon Cheese Pressed Cookies (above)—except omit lemon juice and rind. Add 2 sq. unsweetened chocolate (2 oz.), melted, after the egg.

VIENNESE SHORTBREAD

A special-occasion cooky . . . tender strips made with your cooky press put together with a coffee-flavored filling. Shared with us by Sheila John.

1 cup butter or margarine	2 cups all-purpose flour
½ cup sifted confectioners' sugar	¼ tsp. baking powder
½ tsp. vanilla	Mocha Filling (below)

Heat oven to 375° (quick mod.). Cream butter, confectioners' sugar, and vanilla until fluffy. Measure flour by dipping method (p. 5) or by sifting. Blend flour and baking powder; stir into butter mixture. Using medium star design in cooky press, press out strips, 3" long, on ungreased baking sheet, placing about an inch apart. (If dough does not come through press smoothly, add 1 or 2 tsp. cream.) Bake about 7 min., or until very lightly browned around the edges. Cool. Put 2 cookies together with Filling. For a fancier trim, the ends of cookies may be dipped in sweet chocolate. *Makes about 2 doz. double cookies.*

Note: *If you use self-rising flour, omit baking powder.*

Mocha Filling: Mix ⅔ cup sifted confectioners' sugar, 2 tbsp. soft butter or margarine, and 1 tsp. powdered instant coffee dissolved in 1 tsp. boiling water until fluffy. If too dry, add a few drops of water.

Peanut Butter Fingers (above)

Lemon Cheese Pressed Cookies (above)

Viennese Shortbread (above)

How to Make Perfect Molded Cookies

Mix dough as directed. Richer, softer doughs call for chilling before shaping. Roll into balls between palms of hands. Bake as balls or flatten with bottom of glass or by crisscrossing with fork.

For attractive crescents, fruits, candy canes, etc., take your time and mold cookies carefully. As you become more skillful, molding will go more quickly.

Perfect molded cookies have:
- *uniform shape*
- *delicate brown exterior*
- *crisp, tender eating quality*
- *pleasing flavor*

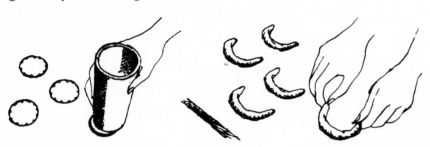

SNICKERDOODLES

The recipe for this delicious "family cooky" came to us from Mrs. Ronald Anfinson, Benson, Minnesota.

1 cup shortening (part butter or margarine)	2 tsp. cream of tartar
	1 tsp. soda
	¼ tsp. salt
1½ cups sugar	2 tbsp. sugar
2 eggs	2 tsp. cinnamon
2¾ cups all-purpose flour	

Heat oven to 400° (mod. hot). Mix shortening, 1½ cups sugar, and eggs thoroughly. Measure flour by dipping method (p. 5) or by sifting. Blend flour, cream of tartar, soda, and salt; stir in. Shape dough in 1" balls. Roll in mixture of 2 tbsp. sugar and cinnamon. Place 2" apart on ungreased baking sheet. Bake 8 to 10 min. These cookies puff up at first, then flatten out. *Makes 6 doz. cookies.*

Note: *If you use self-rising flour, omit cream of tartar, soda, and salt.*

CHOCOLATE CRINKLES

See color picture, pp. 50-51.

½ cup vegetable oil	2 tsp. vanilla
4 sq. unsweetened chocolate (4 oz.), melted	2 cups all-purpose flour
	2 tsp. baking powder
2 cups granulated sugar	½ tsp. salt
4 eggs	1 cup confectioners' sugar

Mix oil, chocolate, and granulated sugar. Blend in one egg at a time until well mixed. Add vanilla. Measure flour by dipping method (p. 5) or by sifting. Stir flour, baking powder, and salt into oil mixture. Chill several hours or overnight.

Heat oven to 350° (mod.). Drop teaspoonfuls of dough into confectioners' sugar. Roll in sugar; shape into balls. Place 2" apart on greased baking sheet. Bake 10 to 12 min., or until almost no imprint remains when touched lightly in center. *Makes 6 doz. cookies.*

Note: *If you use self-rising flour, omit baking powder and salt.*

Snickerdoodles (above)

Shamrock Cookies (p. 29)

Chocolate Crinkles (above)

PEANUT BUTTER COOKIES

So rich, good with anything; a favorite with men and children. Many homemakers double the recipe since these cookies disappear quickly.

½ cup shortening (half butter or margarine)	1 egg
½ cup peanut butter	1¼ cups all-purpose flour
½ cup granulated sugar	½ tsp. baking powder
½ cup brown sugar (packed)	¾ tsp. soda
	¼ tsp. salt

Mix shortening, peanut butter, sugars, and egg thoroughly. Measure flour by dipping method (p. 5) or by sifting. Blend all dry ingredients; stir into shortening mixture. Chill dough.

Heat oven to 375° (quick mod.). Roll dough in 1¼″ balls. Place 3″ apart on lightly greased baking sheet. Flatten crisscross style with fork dipped in flour. Bake 10 to 12 min. *Makes about 3 doz. 2½″ cookies.*

Note: *If you use self-rising flour, omit baking powder, soda, and salt.*

HONEY PEANUT BUTTER COOKIES

Make Peanut Butter Cookies (above)—except use only ¼ cup shortening and use ½ cup honey in place of brown sugar.

PEANUT BUTTER AND JELLY COOKIES

Make dough for Peanut Butter Cookies (above). Chill.

Heat oven to 375°. Shape dough in 1″ balls. Roll in ½ cup finely chopped peanuts. Place about 3″ apart on baking sheet; press thumb gently in center of each. Bake 10 to 12 min. Spoon small amount of jelly or preserves in thumbprint.

PECAN SPICE COOKIES

½ cup shortening (half butter or margarine	½ tsp. salt
	½ tsp. ginger
1¼ cups brown sugar (packed)	½ tsp. cinnamon
	½ tsp. cloves
1 egg	½ tsp. nutmeg
1¾ cups all-purpose flour	⅓ cup chopped pecans
2 tsp. baking powder	4 to 5 doz. pecan halves (for tops)

Heat oven to 375° (quick mod.). Mix shortening, sugar, and egg thoroughly. Measure flour by dipping method (p. 5) or by sifting. Blend dry ingredients; stir into shortening mixture. Stir in chopped pecans. Roll dough in 1″ balls. Place 2″ apart on greased baking sheet. Place a pecan half on top of each cooky, flattening slightly. Bake 10 to 12 min. For softer cookies, store in tight container with an apple slice. *Makes 4 to 5 doz. cookies.*

Note: *If you use self-rising flour, omit baking powder and salt.*

Peanut Butter Cookies (above)

Candy Cane Cookies (p. 37)

Gingersnaps (p. 102)

RUSSIAN TEACAKES

Sometimes called Mexican Wedding Cakes. See color picture, pp. 50-51.

1 cup butter
   or margarine
	2¼ cups all-purpose
	   flour

½ cup sifted confec- tioners' sugar	¼ tsp. salt
1 tsp. vanilla	¾ cup finely chopped nuts

Mix butter, sugar, and vanilla thoroughly. Measure flour by dipping method (p. 5) or by sifting. Stir flour and salt together; blend in. Mix in nuts. Chill dough.

Heat oven to 400° (mod. hot). Roll dough in 1" balls. Place on ungreased baking sheet. (Cookies do not spread.) Bake 10 to 12 min., or until set but not brown. While still warm, roll in confectioners' sugar. Cool. Roll in sugar again. *Makes about 4 doz. 1" cookies.*

Note: *Do not use self-rising flour in this recipe.*

BRIEF MOMENTS

Make dough for Russian Teacakes (above) omitting nuts. Form ½ teaspoonfuls of dough into kiss shape. Bake in 400° oven 8 to 10 min. When cool, put two together (flat sides) with tinted Easy Creamy Icing (p. 150). *Makes 7 doz. cookies.*

COCKLE SHELLS

Make dough for Russian Teacakes (above) omitting nuts. Divide dough in half. Color half coral (¼ tsp. red food coloring and 7 drops yellow food coloring); leave remaining half white. Chill dough. Put together 1 level tsp. coral dough and 1 level tsp. white dough. Roll into pencil-like roll. (If dough becomes soft or sticky, roll on lightly floured surface.) Shape roll in a coil on baking sheet. Bake about 8 min. *Makes 40 cockle shells.*

DATE-OATMEAL COOKIES

Try these golden crispy rounds for a pleasant change from the old standby, oatmeal-raisin cookies.

¾ cup shortening
   (half butter or
   margarine)
	2 cups all-purpose
	   flour

1 cup brown sugar (packed)	¾ tsp. soda
2 eggs	1 tsp. salt
3 tbsp. milk	2 cups rolled oats
1 tsp. vanilla	1½ cups cut-up dates
	¾ cup chopped nuts

Mix shortening, sugar, eggs, milk, and vanilla thoroughly. Measure flour by dipping method (p. 5) or by sifting. Blend flour, soda, and salt; stir in. Mix in oats, dates, and nuts. Chill.

Heat oven to 375° (quick mod.). Roll dough in 1¼" balls. Place 3" apart on lightly greased baking sheet. Flatten to ¼" thickness with bottom of glass dipped in flour. Bake 10 to 12 min., or until lightly browned. *Makes 4 doz. 2½" cookies.*

Note: *If you use self-rising flour, omit soda and salt.*

Cockle Shells
(above)

Cooky-Candies
(p. 38)

Russian
Teacakes
(above)

COCONUT BUTTER BALLS

Rich cooky dough molded around a pecan . . . topped with coconut. For variety, use whole blanched almonds, dates, or candy-coated chocolate candy.

1 cup butter or margarine	2 cups (½ lb.) pecan halves
½ cup sugar	1 egg white
2 tsp. vanilla	1 tbsp. water
2 cups all-purpose flour	¾ to 1 cup flaked coconut
¼ tsp. salt	

Heat oven to 350° (mod.). Cream butter, sugar, and vanilla until fluffy. Measure flour by dipping method (p. 5) or by sifting. Blend flour and salt; stir into creamed mixture, blending thoroughly. If dough is soft, chill until firm enough to shape. With fingers, shape a rounded teaspoonful of dough around each pecan half (cut very large pecan halves in two) to form 1″ balls. Beat egg white and water with fork. Dip dough in egg white mixture, then in coconut. Bake on lightly greased baking sheet 15 to 18 min., or until lightly browned. (These cookies store well if kept in a tightly covered container.) *Makes 5 doz. cookies.*

Note: *If you use self-rising flour, omit salt.*

BRAZILIAN COFFEE COOKIES

A gingersnap-type cooky with real coffee flavor.

⅓ cup shortening	2 cups all-purpose flour
½ cup brown sugar (packed)	½ tsp. salt
½ cup granulated sugar	¼ tsp. soda
1 egg	¼ tsp. baking powder
1½ tsp. vanilla	2 tbsp. powdered instant coffee
1 tbsp. milk	

Heat oven to 400° (mod. hot). Mix shortening, sugars, egg, vanilla, and milk until fluffy. Measure flour by dipping method (p. 5) or by sifting. Stir dry ingredients together. Add to sugar mixture; mix thoroughly. Shape dough in 1″ balls. If dough is too soft, chill until easy to handle. Place balls 2″ apart on ungreased baking sheet. Flatten to ⅛″ thickness with greased fork dipped in sugar (press only in one direction) or with greased bottom of glass dipped in sugar. Bake 8 to 10 min., or until lightly browned. *Makes 4 doz. cookies.*

Note: *If you use self-rising flour, omit salt, soda, and baking powder.*

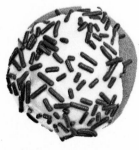

Bonbon Cookies (p. 148)

Coconut Butter Balls (above)

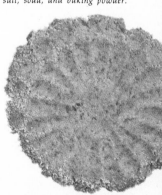

Brazilian Coffee Cookies (above)

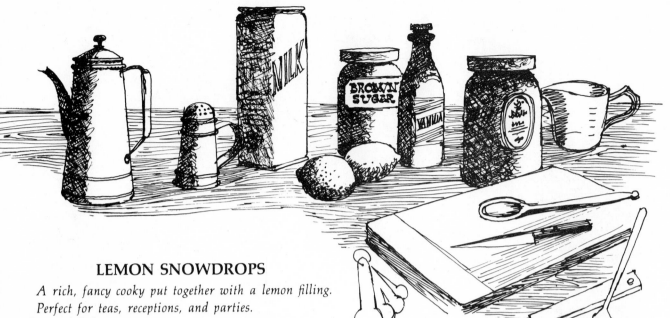

LEMON SNOWDROPS

A rich, fancy cooky put together with a lemon filling. Perfect for teas, receptions, and parties.

1 cup butter or margarine	**2 cups all-purpose flour**
½ cup sifted confectioners' sugar	**¼ tsp. salt**
1 tsp. lemon extract	**Lemon Butter Filling (below)**

Heat oven to 400° (mod. hot). Cream butter and sugar. Measure flour by dipping method (p. 5) or by sifting. Add lemon extract, flour, and salt; mix well. Measure level teaspoonfuls of dough; round into balls and flatten slightly. Place about 1" apart on ungreased baking sheet. Bake 8 to 10 min., or until very lightly browned. Cool. Put together with Filling. Roll in confectioners' sugar. *Makes about 4 doz. double cookies.*

Note: *If you use self-rising flour, omit salt.*

Lemon Butter Filling: Mix ½ cup sugar, 2 tbsp. cornstarch, and dash salt. Add ½ cup water, 2 tbsp. butter, 2 tsp. grated lemon rind, 3 tbsp. lemon juice, and 3 drops yellow food coloring. Bring to rolling boil, stirring constantly; boil and stir 1 min. Cool.

WUNDER-BAR COOKIES

Be sure to bake long enough to lightly brown.

1 cup butter or margarine	**2 cups all-purpose flour**
¾ cup sifted confectioners' sugar	**½ cup light cream**
1½ tsp. vanilla	**½ cup pecans or walnuts, coarsely chopped**

Cream butter, sugar, and vanilla together. Measure flour by dipping method (p. 5) or by sifting. Stir in flour alternately with cream. Blend in nuts. Chill dough thoroughly.

Heat oven to 350° (mod.). Shape in 1" balls. Place on ungreased baking sheet. Bake about 20 min., or until lightly browned. *Makes about 6 doz. cookies.*

Thumbprint Cookies (p. 77)

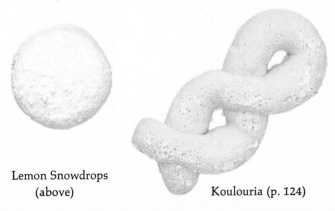

Lemon Snowdrops (above)

Koulouria (p. 124)

Holiday Cookies

The cooky is traditionally associated with the holiday, or holy day, in every land on earth. A sweet that fits the hand, a finger food, an ornament, a good-luck charm—the cooky takes many shapes and endless flavorings. Simple, edible, a warm-hearted gift because it is handmade, the cooky is a symbol of our childlike delight in festivals and sociability. Not only at Christmas time, but also around the calendar, let cooky baking become a happy holiday custom in your home. Celebrate the religious, the patriotic, or the sentimental dates of the year with the time-honored observance of a special "something good to eat."

VALENTINE'S DAY

On this sentimental day, when Hearts and Flowers rule, revive the delightful old-fashioned custom of baking a sweet cooky message to express your love.

LOVE LETTERS

Our adaptation of an old German cooky. Perfect for St. Valentine's Day entertaining, for engagement parties, or for bridal showers.

2 cups all-purpose flour
½ cup sugar
1 tsp. salt
1 cup butter or margarine
2 tsp. finely grated lemon rind
finely grated rind of 1 orange
½ cup commercial sour cream

Heat oven to 475° (very hot). Measure flour by dipping method (p. 5) or by sifting. Blend flour, sugar, and salt. Cut in butter and rinds until mixture resembles coarse meal. Blend sour cream in evenly. Gather dough into firm ball. Divide in half. Roll on well-floured board to ⅛" thickness. Cut in 3x2" pieces; fold ends to center, overlapping slightly; seal with tiny piece of candied cherry. Place on ungreased baking sheet. Brush tops with water; sprinkle with sugar. Bake 6 to 8 min. *Makes about 4 doz. cookies.*

Note: *If you use self-rising flour, omit salt.*

HEART COOKIES

Roll dough for Mary's Sugar Cookies (p. 18) 1/16" thick. Cut in heart shapes. Bake. Cool. Frost with pink-tinted Easy Creamy Icing (p. 150), or put 2 baked heart-shaped cookies together with red-tinted peppermint-flavored icing.

ST. PATRICK'S DAY

Let the wearing of the green come right through to your baking. These Luck o' the Irish cookies make a grand St. Patrick's Day surprise for the whole family.

SHAMROCK COOKIES

Faith and begorra, they're good! Wonderful for parties or lunchboxes.

1 cup shortening (half butter or margarine)
1 cup sifted confectioners' sugar
1 egg
1 to 2 tsp. peppermint flavoring
2½ cups all-purpose flour
1 tsp. salt
1½ tsp. green food coloring

Heat oven to 375° (quick mod.). Mix shortening, sugar, egg, and flavoring thoroughly. Measure flour by dipping method (p. 5) or by sifting. Stir in flour, salt, and food coloring. To shape shamrocks, roll 3 small balls (¼ tsp. dough each); flatten together with fingertip into shamrock shape; shape stem and attach. Sprinkle with green decorators' sugar. Complete cookies one at a time or the tiny balls may become dry and crack when pressed. Bake about 9 min. *Makes 9 doz. cookies.*

Note: *If you use self-rising flour, omit salt.*

GOOD LUCK COOKIES

Make Shamrock Cookies (above)—except make 4 small balls for each cooky; shape them into four-leaf clovers.

SHAMROCK CUT-OUTS

Follow directions for a favorite sugar cooky dough recipe, such as Mary's Sugar Cookies (p. 18); cut out using club cutter. Bake and frost with green-tinted icing.

Spring's return and the religious festival of the Resurrection are traditionally observed by Easter bakings made from treasured recipes . . . while youngsters love any cooky in the shapes of rabbits and eggs.

GREEK EASTER COOKIES

The Greeks call these tender clove-flavored cookies Kourabiedes. See color picture, p. 122.

1 cup butter or margarine	1 tsp. vanilla
⅓ cup granulated sugar	2 cups all-purpose flour
2 egg yolks	1 tsp. baking powder
½ tsp. brandy flavoring, if desired	1 tsp. cloves confectioners' sugar

Heat oven to 350° (mod.). Mix the first 5 ingredients together thoroughly. Measure flour by dipping method (p. 5) or by sifting. Blend flour, baking powder, and cloves; stir into butter mixture; mix well. Shape dough in small balls, about ¾" in diameter, or in cylindrical shapes formed in 2" long half-moons. Place cookies on lightly greased baking sheet. Bake 10 to 12 min., or until cookies are set but not browned. Let stand 2 min. before removing from baking sheet. When cool, dust with confectioners' sugar. (For a more authentic Greek cooky, omit ground cloves and place a whole clove in center of each cooky before baking.) *Makes 8 doz. cookies.*

Note: *If you use self-rising flour, omit baking powder.*

EASTER EGGS

Make favorite sugar cooky dough. Make your own egg cooky cutter: squeeze or press an empty frozen juice or soup can —both ends removed—into an oval shape. Cut egg shapes; bake. Decorate as desired with pastel-tinted icing.

When the pumpkin's carved and lighted, the masks are off, and everyone gathers 'round the crackling fire to shiver at ghostly tales of goblins, serve this wholesome cooky treat—a quick and easy trick to make.

PUMPKIN COOKIES

1½ cups brown sugar (packed)	1 tbsp. baking powder
½ cup shortening	1 tsp. cinnamon
2 eggs	½ tsp. nutmeg
1¾ cups canned pumpkin	½ tsp. salt
2¾ cups all-purpose flour	¼ tsp. ginger
	1 cup raisins
	1 cup chopped pecans

Heat oven to 400° (mod. hot). Mix sugar, shortening, eggs, and pumpkin thoroughly. Measure flour by dipping method (p. 5) or by sifting. Blend dry ingredients; add to pumpkin mixture, stirring until well blended. Add raisins and pecans. Drop batter by teaspoonfuls on ungreased baking sheet. Bake 12 to 15 min., or until lightly browned. Cookies may be iced when cool with a thin butter icing. *Makes about 6 doz. cookies.*

Note: *If you use self-rising flour, omit baking powder and salt.*

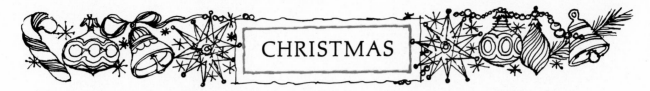

CHRISTMAS

'Tis the season to be jolly, 'tis the season of tree-trimming and carol-singing, <u>and</u> the season of cooky baking. Whether you're baking two or three specialties for family enjoyment or a wide variety for gift boxes, we suggest starting early so that you can be free to take part in all the activities of the holiday. And do let the children help; what pride they take in serving cookies they have cut and decorated.

MERRY CHRISTMAS COOKIES

See color picture, pp. 32-33.

⅓ cup shortening	2¾ cups all-purpose
⅓ cup sugar	flour
1 egg	1 tsp. soda
⅔ cup honey	1 tsp. salt
1 tsp. lemon flavoring	

Mix shortening, sugar, egg, honey, and flavoring thoroughly. Measure flour by dipping method (p. 5) or by sifting. Stir together flour, soda, salt; blend in. Chill dough.

Heat oven to 375° (quick mod.). Roll dough out ¼" thick. Cut into desired shapes (right). Place 1" apart on lightly greased baking sheet. Bake 8 to 10 min., or until no imprint remains when touched lightly. When cool, ice and decorate as desired. *Makes about 5 doz. 2½" cookies.*

Note: *If you use self-rising flour, omit salt; reduce soda to ¼ tsp.*

MERRY CHRISTMAS MOLASSES COOKIES

Make Merry Christmas Cookies (above)—except use brown sugar in place of granulated, molasses in place of honey, and 2 tsp. cinnamon plus 1 tsp. ginger in place of lemon flavoring. Shape and decorate (below).

Toys: Outline shapes (drum, car, jack-in-the-box, etc.) with white or colored icing. Pipe icing on animals (reindeer, elephant, horse, camel, dog, kitten, etc.) to give effect of bridles, blankets, or saddles.

Boys and Girls: Pipe figures with an icing to give desired effects: eyes, noses, buttons, etc.

TO DECORATE

Use recipe for Easy Creamy Icing (p. 150). Colored or white sugar in coarse granules for decorating is available at your grocery store.

Wreaths: Cut dough with scalloped cutter, using smaller cutter for center. Cover with white icing. Sprinkle with green sugar and decorate with clusters of berries made of red icing—leaves of green icing—to give effect of holly wreaths.

Bells: Outline and make clapper with red icing.

Stockings: Sprinkle colored sugar on toes and heels before baking. Or mark heels and toes of baked cookies with icing of some contrasting color.

Santa Clauses: Outline with red icing. Fill bag with tiny candies. Paint boots with melted chocolate.

Angels: Frost skirt and face white; wings light blue. Trim with gold or silver dragées.

Christmas Trees: Spread with white icing. Sprinkle with green sugar. Decorate with silver dragées and tiny colored candies.

Coconut Chews (p. 109)

Holiday Spritz (p. 21)

Merry Christmas Cookies (this page)

Chocolate Spritz (p. 21)

(See color picture on following pages.)

POINSETTIA AND HOLLY COOKIES

The brilliant red of the Christmas poinsettia or the deep green of the holly leaf makes the perfect accent for holiday cooky plates.

Make dough for Merry Christmas Cookies (p. 31); chill. Heat oven to 375° (quick mod.). Roll ½ the dough out ¼″ thick on lightly floured cloth-covered board; make Poinsettia or Holly Leaves (below). Use remaining dough for rolled cookies of your choice.

For Poinsettia: Using a sharp knife, cut from rolled dough a poinsettia petal 4 to 5″ long and about 1¼″ wide. (Cut gently so cloth isn't cut.) One end of petal should be gently rounded; the other should come to a slim point. Repeat, making 7 petals. (Poinsettia will be more realistic looking if petals are not identical in shape and size.) Place on lightly greased baking sheet. Bake 8 to 10 min. When cool, ice petals with Red Icing: mix 15 drops (scant ¼ tsp.) red food coloring and 2 drops yellow food coloring into half the Decorator Icing (below). Arrange the 7 poinsettia petals in a circle in center of tray of holiday cookies.

For Holly Leaves: With round edge of 1 tbsp. measuring spoon, cut about 12 holly leaves from remaining rolled dough. Each cut of the spoon will make one scallop of the holly leaf. Make holly leaves different sizes—some smaller, some larger. Place on lightly greased baking sheet; bake 8 to 10 min. When cool, ice leaves with Green Icing: mix 10 drops green food coloring into half the Decorator Icing (below). For holly berries, place 3 red cinnamon candies (red hots) on one corner of each green iced holly leaf. Use leaves to garnish tray of Christmas cookies or to add color to a gift box of Christmas cookies.

Decorator Icing: Blend ½ cup confectioners' sugar, ¼ tsp. vanilla, and 1½ to 2 tsp. cream. Divide in half.

CHRISTMAS BELLS

Rich, delicious cookies . . . and most attractive. See color picture below and on p. 36.

½ cup shortening (part butter or margarine)	1 tsp. vanilla
½ cup sugar	1½ cups all-purpose flour
1 egg	¼ tsp. soda
	½ tsp. salt

Mix shortening, sugar, egg, and vanilla thoroughly. Measure flour by dipping method (p. 5) or by sifting. Stir flour, soda, and salt together; blend in. Color ⅔ of the dough red or green. Mold into 10x1½″ roll. Mold this roll into a bell shape by squeezing the top together and leaving the lower half flared and curving; chill. Save ¼ cup white dough for clappers. Roll out rest of dough on waxed paper into rectangle large enough to cover colored roll, about 10x4″; trim edges. Wrap around roll (see picture); chill again.

Heat oven to 375° (quick mod.). Cut ⅛″ thick slices. Place ½″ apart on ungreased baking sheet. Press tiny ball of dough at bottom for clapper. Bake 8 to 10 min. *Makes 5 doz. cookies.*

Note: *If you use self-rising flour, omit soda and salt.*

CHRISTMAS BALLS

Make Christmas Bells (above)—except leave roll round (do not shape bell); after adding outside strip of white, roll in colored shot.

WONDERLAND COOKIES

For a Christmas tree with old-fashioned charm, trim the tree with these colorful and unusual cookies.

½ cup butter or margarine	**2½ cups all-purpose flour**
1 cup sugar	**½ tsp. salt**
2 eggs	**¼ tsp. soda**
2 tbsp. cream	**food coloring**
1 tsp. vanilla	

Mix butter, sugar, and eggs thoroughly. Stir in cream and vanilla. Measure flour by dipping method (p. 5) or by sifting. Stir dry ingredients together; blend in. Tint dough with food coloring as desired. Chill dough 4 to 5 hr. or overnight.

Heat oven to 400° (mod. hot). Roll dough a little at a time ⅛" thick on well-floured cloth-covered board. (Keep rest chilled.) Cut out cookies as directed for special shapes (right). Place on ungreased baking sheet. Bake 6 to 8 min., or until delicately browned. Let stand a minute before removing from baking sheet. If desired, decorate with Easy Creamy Icing (p. 150) or colored sugar. *Makes 4 to 5 doz. cookies.*

Note: *If you use self-rising flour, omit salt and soda.*

MAGIC RINGS

Using doughnut cutter or fluted cutters, make two rings for each cooky. Bake a few cookies at a time. Immediately after baking, place cookies on towel and slit top of every other one. Slip an uncut cooky ring through opening while still warm (see below).

CHRISTMAS TREE BALLS

Color part of dough red and part green with food coloring, leaving some white. Cut white and colored rings with doughnut cutter. Fit white centers into colored rings and colored centers into white and colored rings (see below). Press ends of 4 to 6" long string firmly into cooky. Sprinkle with white and colored sugars; bake.

MOBILE STARS

Cut two stars for each cooky. Put 6" loop of cord on baking sheet. Press two adjoining points of one star firmly on two ends of cord, extending cord halfway into points for solid fastening. Between the two points, cut slit past center (see below). Spread to ¼" opening. Slit second cooky. Bake and, if desired, decorate. Fit baked stars together at opening (also below). If slit bakes together, cut and spread apart while cookies are warm.

Merry Maker Cookies
(this page)

Christmas Bells
(p. 34)

Spritz (p. 21)

Sandbakelser (p. 44)

Candy Cane Cookies
(this page)

Thumbprint Cookies (p. 77)

A PARTY IDEA

A popular once-a-year party is the Christ-mas cooky swap party. Friends and neighbors gather, each bringing one dozen of her holiday specialty for each woman at the party. Cookies are set out to sample and admire and coffee is served. Afterward each one takes home a wonderful variety of festive cookies. See color picture opposite.

MERRY MAKER COOKIES

See color picture opposite.

Make dough for Mary's Sugar Cookies (p. 18). Divide dough into several parts. Tint each part a different color: use liquid food coloring for delicate colors; use paste coloring for deeper colors (paste colors are available through mail-order baking equipment stores). Rolling dough ⅛" thick, roll several colored doughs together to make patchwork; cut with cooky cutters. Or roll each color out separately; cut with sharp knife or cutters and fit pieces together to make designs.

Heat oven to 375° (quick mod.). Place cookies on lightly greased baking sheet. Bake 7 to 8 min., or until delicately golden. *Makes about 4 doz. cookies.*

CHRISTMAS HOLLI-DOODLES

Make Snickerdoodles (p. 23)—except instead of rolling in cinnamon and sugar, roll in red or green decorators' sugar.

CANDY CANE COOKIES

See color picture opposite.

1 cup shortening (half butter or margarine)	2½ cups all-purpose flour
1 cup sifted confectioners' sugar	1 tsp. salt
	½ tsp. red food coloring
1 egg	½ cup crushed peppermint candy
1½ tsp. almond extract	
1 tsp. vanilla	½ cup granulated sugar

Heat oven to 375° (quick mod.). Mix shortening, sugar, egg, and flavorings thoroughly. Measure flour by dipping method (p. 5) or by sifting. Mix flour and salt; stir into shortening mixture. Divide dough in half. Blend food coloring into one half.

Roll a 4" strip (using 1 tsp. dough) from each color. For smooth, even strips, roll them back and forth on lightly floured board. Place strips side by side, press lightly together and twist like rope (see sketch). For best results, complete cookies one at a time—if all the dough of one color is shaped first, strips become too dry to twist. Place on ungreased baking sheet. Curve top to form handle of cane.

Bake about 9 min., until lightly browned. While still warm, sprinkle with mixture of candy and sugar. *Makes about 4 doz. canes.*

Note: *If you use self-rising flour, omit salt.*

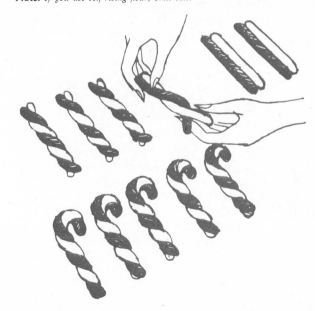

CREAM FILBERT CANDY COOKIES

A Christmas cooky that resembles creamed filberts (mothball candies).

1 cup shortening (part butter or margarine)	⅛ tsp. salt
	1 tsp. vanilla
¾ cup sugar	2 to 3 oz. filberts
1 egg	Glaze (below)
2½ cups all-purpose flour	60 sugar cubes, crushed, or coarse granulated sugar
½ tsp. baking powder	

Heat oven to 375° (quick mod.). Cream shortening and sugar. Add egg. Measure flour by dipping method (p. 5) or by sifting. Stir dry ingredients together. Blend into creamed mixture. Add vanilla. Roll in balls (using 1 level tsp. dough per ball) and press a filbert in center. Shape so dough covers nut. Place on ungreased baking sheet about 2″ apart. Bake 12 to 15 min., until delicately browned. Cool. Holding cooky at bottom, dip entire top in Glaze. Roll cooky in crushed sugar. *Makes 7 to 8 doz. cookies.*

Note: *If you use self-rising flour, omit baking powder and salt.*

Glaze: Mix 2 cups sifted confectioners' sugar, 3 tbsp. water, and 2 tsp. vanilla.

COOKY-CANDIES

Rich oatmeal shortbread-type cooky with festive toppings. Also called Sprinkle-Top Cookies.

1 cup butter or margarine	½ cup rolled oats
¾ cup sifted confectioners' sugar	½ cup semi-sweet chocolate pieces
1 tbsp. vanilla	¼ cup milk
2 cups all-purpose flour	finely chopped pecans
¾ tsp. salt	shredded coconut
	chocolate shot

Heat oven to 325° (slow mod.). Mix butter, sugar, and vanilla well. Measure flour by dipping method (p. 5) or by sifting. Stir flour, salt, and rolled oats into butter mixture.

With fingers, shape teaspoonfuls of dough into rounds, balls, crescents, triangles, and bars. Bake on ungreased baking sheet 20 to 25 min., or until golden around edges. (Watch baking time. These are easily overbaked.) Cool.

Melt chocolate; add milk; blend until smooth. Dip cookies, rounded-side-down, in chocolate; then dip in nuts, coconut, or chocolate shot. *Makes about 4 doz. cookies.*

Note: *Do not use self-rising flour in this recipe.*

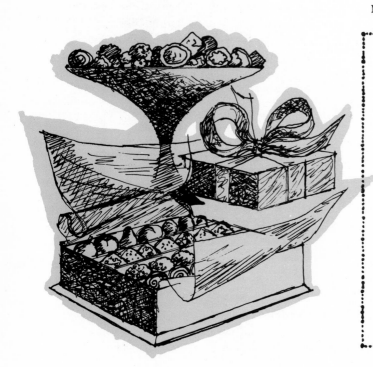

PLAN YOUR CHRISTMAS BAKING

Christmas cookies that are low in shortening, such as Pfeffernüsse (p. 45), Lebkuchen (p. 52), and German Spice Cakes (p. 53), should be baked three to four weeks before the holidays and stored to develop flavor.

Cookies that are rich in fruit, like Holiday Fruit Drops (p. 146), or tender soft cookies may be baked two weeks early. Store them in an airtight container (a covered earthenware jar or a can with a tight cover). A cut piece of apple or orange in the jar helps keep cookies moist; change fruit frequently. Rich butter cookies are best when baked shortly before using. If you have freezer space, they may be baked ahead of time and frozen (see p. 5).

TOFFEE SQUARES

Rich cooky that looks and tastes like toffee candy.

1 cup butter or mar- garine	2 cups all-purpose flour
1 cup brown sugar (packed)	¼ tsp. salt
1 egg yolk	½ milk chocolate bar (8-oz. size)
1 tsp. vanilla	½ cup chopped nuts

Heat oven to 350° (mod.). Mix butter, sugar, egg yolk, and vanilla. Measure flour by dipping method (p. 5) or by sifting. Stir in flour and salt until dough is well blended. Spread in a rectangle about 13x10" on greased baking sheet, leaving about 1" all around edge of baking sheet. Bake 20 to 25 min., or until nicely browned. (For a softer cake-like cooky, spread dough in an oblong pan, 13x9½x2"; bake 25 to 30 min.) Crust will still be soft. Remove from oven. Immediately place separated pieces of chocolate on top. Let stand until soft; spread evenly over entire surface. Sprinkle with nuts. Cut in small squares while warm. *Makes 6 to 7 doz. squares.*

Note: *If you use self-rising flour, omit salt.*

BUTTERSCOTCH TOFFEE SQUARES

Make Toffee Squares (above)—except while crust bakes, melt and blend 1 pkg. (6 oz.) butterscotch pieces, ¼ cup light corn syrup, 2 tbsp. shortening, 1 tbsp. water, and ¼ tsp. salt over hot water. Spread butterscotch mixture (instead of softened chocolate) over entire surface.

SNOWFLAKES

½ cup sugar	½ tsp. baking powder
⅓ cup butter or margarine	½ tsp. salt
1 egg	sweet chocolate, melted
½ tsp. vanilla	pistachio nuts, chopped
1¼ cups all-purpose flour	

Mix sugar, butter, egg, and flavoring well. Measure flour by dipping method (p. 5) or by sifting. Blend dry ingredients into shortening mixture. Chill 1 hr.

Heat oven to 400° (mod. hot). Roll dough ⅛" thick on floured board. Cut into small stars. Bake on ungreased baking sheet 6 to 8 min., until lightly browned. Cool. Put two cookies together with melted sweet chocolate; add dab of chocolate and sprinkling of chopped pistachio nuts on top. *Makes 32 cookies.*

Note: *If you use self-rising flour, omit baking powder and salt.*

CHRISTMAS STOCKINGS

1 cup shortening (part butter)	2¼ cups all-purpose flour
½ cup sifted confec- tioners' sugar	½ tsp. salt
1 tsp. vanilla	9 candied cherries, quartered
½ tsp. almond flavoring	¼ cup broken nuts
¼ to ½ tsp. red or green food coloring	¼ cup semi-sweet chocolate pieces
	Easy Creamy Icing (p. 150)

Mix shortening, sugar, flavorings, and food coloring well. Measure flour by dipping method (p. 5) or by sifting. Blend flour and salt; stir into shortening mixture. Chill 1 hr.

Heat oven to 400° (mod. hot). In palm of hand pat 1 level tbsp. dough into oblong about 3x1½". If dough seems to be too dry, carefully add a few drops of cream. Lengthwise down center, place "surprises"— 2 chocolate pieces, 1 cherry quarter, 2 pieces of nuts. Mold dough around "surprises" and shape into roll 3" long. Place on ungreased baking sheet, turning end of roll to form foot of stocking. Bake 10 to 12 min. Cool. Ice tops and toes. *Makes about 3 doz. stockings.*

Note: *Do not use self-rising flour in this recipe.*

CRANBERRY DROPS

½ cup butter or margarine	3 cups all-purpose flour
1 cup granulated sugar	1 tsp. baking powder
¾ cup brown sugar (packed)	½ tsp. salt
¼ cup milk	¼ tsp. soda
2 tbsp. orange juice	1 cup chopped nuts
1 egg	2½ cups coarsely chopped cranberries

Heat oven to 375° (quick mod.). Cream butter and sugars together. Beat in milk, orange juice, and egg. Measure flour by dipping method (p. 5) or by sifting. Stir together flour, baking powder, salt, and soda. Blend well with sugar mixture. Stir in chopped nuts and cranberries. Drop dough by teaspoonfuls on greased baking sheet. Bake 10 to 15 min. *Makes 11 doz. cookies.*

Note: *If you use self-rising flour, omit baking powder, salt, and soda.*

CREAM WAFERS

Delicate pastry-like rounds with a rich filling. A lovely addition to the cooky trays for a tea or reception. See color picture, p. 46.

1 cup butter or margarine	2 cups all-purpose flour
⅓ cup whipping cream (35% butterfat)	granulated sugar Creamy Butter Filling (below)

Measure flour by dipping method (p. 5) or by sifting. Mix butter, cream, and flour thoroughly. Chill 1 hr.

Heat oven to 375° (quick mod.). Roll dough ⅛″ thick on lightly floured board. Cut into 1½″ rounds. Transfer to waxed paper heavily sprinkled with sugar, turning to coat both sides. Place on ungreased baking sheet. Prick in 4 places with fork. Bake 7 to 9 min., or until slightly puffy. Put two cooled cookies together with Filling. *Makes about 5 doz. 1½″ cookies.*

Note: *You may use self-rising flour in this recipe.*

Creamy Butter Filling: Blend ¼ cup soft butter, ¾ cup sifted confectioners' sugar, and 1 tsp. vanilla. If desired, tint pink or green.

SATIN-GLAZED DATE DROPS

¼ cup butter or margarine	1¼ cups all-purpose flour
¾ cup brown sugar (packed)	½ tsp. soda
1 egg	¼ tsp. baking powder
½ tsp. vanilla	½ cup chopped walnuts
½ cup commercial sour cream	1 lb. soft pitted dates (48)
	Satin Glaze (below)

Heat oven to 400° (mod. hot). Mix butter, sugar, egg, and vanilla until fluffy. Stir in sour cream. Measure flour by dipping method (p. 5) or by sifting. Blend dry ingredients; mix into sugar mixture. Stir in nuts and dates. If dates are large, cut them in half before adding to dough and use half as many. Drop by teaspoonfuls (1 date in each cooky) on lightly greased baking sheet. Bake about 10 min. Cool and frost with Glaze. *Makes about 4 doz. cookies.*

Note: *If you use self-rising flour, omit soda and baking powder.*

Satin Glaze: Heat ½ cup butter or margarine over medium heat until lightly browned but not burned. Remove from heat. Stir in 3 cups sifted confectioners' sugar and 1 tsp. vanilla. Add 3 to 4 tbsp. hot water gradually until glaze is thin spreading consistency.

FROZEN FRUIT COOKIES

1 cup butter or margarine	½ cup pecans, chopped
1 cup sifted confectioners' sugar	½ cup chopped candied fruit or citron
1 egg	1 cup whole candied fruit, such as cherries
2¼ cups all-purpose flour	
¼ tsp. cream of tartar	

Cream butter and sugar together; beat in the egg. Measure flour by dipping method (p. 5) or by sifting. Stir in flour and cream of tartar. Blend in pecans and fruit. Form in rolls 1½″ in diameter. Wrap in foil or transparent plastic wrap; freeze.

Heat oven to 375° (quick mod.). Slice very thinly. Place on greased baking sheet. Bake 6 to 8 min. *Makes about 10 doz. cookies.*

Note: *You may use self-rising flour in this recipe.*

WHITE FRUIT BARS

⅔ cup shortening
½ cup sugar
2 eggs, separated
1 tbsp. sherry
    flavoring
¼ tsp. almond
    flavoring
1¾ cups all-purpose
    flour
2 tsp. baking powder
1 tsp. salt

1 cup cream (20%
    butterfat)
½ cup flaked coconut
¼ cup chopped
    citron
½ cup chopped
    blanched
    almonds
¼ cup cut-up pecans
Easy Creamy Icing
    (p. 150)

Heat oven to 400° (mod. hot). Mix together shortening, sugar, egg yolks, and flavoring until fluffy. Measure flour by dipping method (p. 5) or by sifting. Blend dry ingredients and add alternately with cream to the shortening mixture, starting and ending with dry ingredients. Mix only enough to blend after each addition. Stir in coconut, citron, and nuts. Beat egg whites until stiff; fold into dough. Spread in greased oblong pan, 13x9½x2". Bake about 30 min. Spread with Icing while still warm. When cool, cut into bars. Cookies improve with mellowing; so bake at least 24 hr. before serving. *Makes 2½ to 3 doz. bars.*

Note: *If you use self-rising flour, omit baking powder and salt.*

CHRISTMAS JEWELS

⅓ cup shortening
¼ cup sugar
½ cup molasses
1 egg
1½ cups all-purpose
    flour
½ tsp. soda
¼ tsp. salt
1 tsp. cinnamon

1 tsp. mace
1 tsp. nutmeg
¼ tsp. ginger
¼ tsp. allspice
2½ cups mixed
    candied fruit
    (about 1 lb.)
2 cups nuts, chopped
    coarsely (about
    ½ lb.)

Heat oven to 325° (slow mod.). Mix shortening, sugar, molasses, and egg. Measure flour by dipping method (p. 5) or by sifting. Stir dry ingredients together; blend into shortening mixture. Stir in fruit and nuts. Drop dough by teaspoonfuls about 1" apart on lightly greased baking sheet. Bake 12 to 15 min. *Makes about 6 doz. cookies.*

Note: *If you use self-rising flour, omit soda and salt.*

CHERRY-COCONUT BARS

1 cup all-purpose
    flour
½ cup butter or
    margarine
3 tbsp. confectioners'
    sugar
2 eggs, slightly beaten
1 cup granulated
    sugar

¼ cup all-purpose
    flour
½ tsp. baking powder
¼ tsp. salt
1 tsp. vanilla
¾ cup chopped nuts
½ cup coconut
½ cup quartered
    maraschino
    cherries

Heat oven to 350° (mod.). Measure flour by dipping method (p. 5) or by sifting. With hands, mix 1 cup flour, butter, and confectioners' sugar until smooth. Spread thin with fingers in ungreased square pan, 8x8x2". Bake about 25 min.

Stir rest of ingredients into eggs. Spread over top of baked pastry (no need to cool). Bake about 25 min. Cool. Cut into bars. *Makes 18 bars.*

Note: *If you use self-rising flour, omit baking powder and salt.*

ZIMTSTERNE

A crisp, spicy cooky with a shiny glazed top. A favorite in Switzerland. See color picture opposite.

3 tbsp. butter or margarine	2½ tsp. baking powder
1½ cups sugar	1¼ tsp. cinnamon
2 whole eggs	¼ tsp. salt
1 egg, separated	¼ tsp. nutmeg
1 tsp. lemon juice	½ cup finely chopped walnuts
2⅓ cups all-purpose flour	

Heat oven to 375° (quick mod.). Mix butter, sugar, 2 whole eggs, 1 egg yolk, and lemon juice until fluffy. Measure flour by dipping method (p. 5) or by sifting. Stir dry ingredients together; blend into sugar mixture. Stir in nuts. Roll dough, ⅓ at a time, to 1/16" thick on lightly floured board. Cut with star cutter. Brush tops of cookies with remaining egg white, beaten until frothy. Bake on lightly greased baking sheet 6 to 8 min. *Makes 6 to 9 doz. cookies, depending on size of cutter.*

Note: *If you use self-rising flour, omit baking powder and salt.*

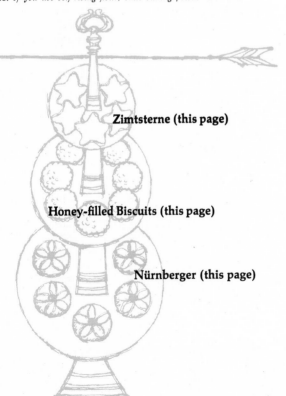

Zimtsterne (this page)

Honey-filled Biscuits (this page)

Nürnberger (this page)

NÜRNBERGER

Almond-decorated honey cookies from the famous German City of Toys. See color picture opposite.

Make Lebkuchen (p. 52)—except in place of honey and molasses, use 1 cup honey. Use only ¼ tsp. cloves, ½ tsp. allspice, and ½ tsp. nutmeg.

Roll out chilled dough ¼" thick on lightly floured board. Cut 2" rounds. Place on greased baking sheet. With fingers, round up cookies a bit toward center. Press in blanched almond halves around the edge like petals of a daisy and a round piece of citron in the center. Bake 10 to 12 min., or just until set. Immediately brush with Glazing Icing (p. 52). Remove from baking sheet. Cool and store to mellow as for Lebkuchen. *Makes 6 doz. cookies.*

HONEY-FILLED BISCUITS

Another unusual and delicious cooky from France . . . often served with cheese. See color picture opposite.

1 cup all-purpose flour	2 egg yolks
¼ cup sugar	1 cup finely chopped candied fruits
¼ tsp. salt	honey
⅓ cup butter or margarine	confectioners' sugar

Measure flour by dipping method (p. 5) or by sifting. Make a well in center of flour in mixing bowl; put in sugar, salt, butter, and egg yolks. Work the ingredients in center into a smooth paste; work in flour until well blended. Mix in fruits. Wrap in waxed paper. Chill 2 hr.

Heat oven to 350° (mod.). Roll dough ⅛" thick on lightly floured board; cut in 2" fluted rounds. Bake on ungreased baking sheet 8 to 10 min., or until tinged with brown. Cool; put together, sandwich-fashion, with honey as filling. Sprinkle tops with confectioners' sugar. *Makes 2 doz. double cookies.*

Note: *If you use self-rising flour, omit salt.*

Easy Shaping Variation: Make dough for Honey-filled Biscuits (above). Divide in half; form 2 rolls, each about 2" across. Chill. Slice very thin; bake.

CINNAMON STARS

Dainty holiday party cookies. Crisp and tender with a slight chewiness and delicate flavor.

⅓ to ½ cup egg whites
2 cups sifted confec-
    tioners' sugar
½ tsp. grated lemon
    rind

½ tsp. cinnamon
2 cups blanched
    almonds
    (½ lb.), ground

Beat egg whites until stiff but not dry. Gradually add sugar and lemon rind. Continue beating until completely blended, about 5 min. Reserve ¾ cup of mixture for centers of cookies. Blend cinnamon and almonds together; fold into remaining egg white mixture. (If batter is too soft for rolling, let stand at room temperature until stiffened to proper consistency.)

Heat oven to 350° (mod.). Using cloth-covered board which has had confectioners' sugar rubbed into the cloth, roll dough ⅛" thick. Cut in star shapes. Place ½ tsp. reserved mixture on center of each star. If desired, spread to each point of star. Place cookies on well-greased and floured baking sheet. Bake about 12 min. *Makes 4½ doz. 2½" cookies.*

SANDBAKELSER

Fragile almond-flavored shells of Swedish origin, made in metal molds of varied designs. Here we call them Sand Tarts. See color picture, p. 36.

⅓ cup blanched
    almonds
4 unblanched almonds
¾ cup butter or
    margarine

¾ cup sugar
1 egg white
1¾ cups all-purpose
    flour

Put almonds through fine knife of food grinder twice (1 tsp. vanilla and 1 tsp. almond flavoring may be substituted for almonds). Mix in butter, sugar, and egg white thoroughly. Measure flour by dipping method (p. 5) or by sifting. Stir in flour. Chill.

Heat oven to 350° (mod.). Press dough into sandbakelse molds (tiny fluted forms) to form thin coating. Place on ungreased baking sheet. Bake 12 to 15 min. Tap molds on table to loosen cookies; turn out. *Makes 3½ doz. cookies.*

Note: *You may use self-rising flour in this recipe.*

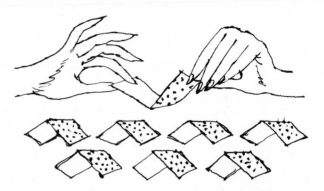

GREEK SESAME SEED COOKIES

A traditional cooky for holidays in the Sparta region of Greece.

1 cup butter or
    margarine
1¾ cups sugar
2 eggs
⅔ cup toasted sesame
    seeds

4 cups all-purpose
    flour
2 tsp. baking powder
½ tsp. salt
¼ cup water

Mix butter, sugar, and eggs until fluffy. Stir in ⅓ cup of the sesame seeds. Measure flour by dipping method (p. 5) or by sifting. Blend dry ingredients; add alternately with water to sugar mixture. Chill dough until stiff enough to roll, 1 to 2 hr.

Heat oven to 350° (mod.). Roll dough on lightly floured board into rectangle ⅛" thick. Cut dough in strips, 2½x¾". Press one entire side of each strip into dish containing the remaining sesame seeds. Loop one end over at right angle to the other, making bowknot effect. Place on lightly greased baking sheet. Bake 8 to 10 min., or until lightly browned. *Makes about 9 doz. cookies.*

Note: *If you use self-rising flour, omit baking powder and salt.*

LIGHT PFEFFERNÜSSE

The light, fruited version of a traditional German Christmas cooky. They may be made larger if you wish. Make them 2 to 3 weeks before Christmas, then mellow by storing with a slice of apple.

3 eggs
1 cup sugar
3 cups all-purpose
    flour
¼ tsp. baking powder
¼ tsp. salt
⅛ tsp. white pepper
1 tsp. cinnamon

⅛ tsp. cloves
¼ cup almonds,
    blanched and
    ground
½ cup chopped
    candied lemon
    or orange peel
    (4-oz. pkg.)

Beat eggs and sugar until frothy. Measure flour by dipping method (p. 5) or by sifting. Blend dry ingredients; stir in. Add almonds and peel. Mix thoroughly with hands. Roll dough ¼" thick on lightly floured board; cut in 1" rounds. Place on lightly greased baking sheet; cover with towel or place in cupboard; leave overnight to dry. (For a softer cooky, do not dry—bake immediately after cutting out.)

Heat oven to 350° (mod.). Bake 20 min., or until lightly browned. *Makes 12 doz. 1" rounds.*

Note: *If you use self-rising flour, omit baking powder and salt.*

DARK PFEFFERNÜSSE

A small, somewhat hard molasses cooky with a mild anise flavor.

½ cup shortening
¾ cup brown sugar
    (packed)
1 egg
½ cup molasses
mixture of 3 drops
    anise oil and 1
    tbsp. hot water

3⅓ cups all-purpose
    flour
½ tsp. soda
¼ tsp. salt
½ tsp. cinnamon
½ tsp. cloves

Heat oven to 350° (mod.). Mix shortening, sugar, egg, molasses, and anise mixture. (Anise oil may be obtained at a pharmacy.) Measure flour by dipping method (p. 5) or by sifting. Blend dry ingredients; mix in gradually with hands. Knead dough until right consistency for molding. If dough seems too soft, refrigerate until firm. Mold into balls ¾" in diameter; place on greased baking sheet. Bake about 12 min., or until golden brown on bottom. Cookies harden on standing. Store in airtight container with slice of apple to mellow them. *Makes 8 doz. cookies.*

Note: *If you use self-rising flour, omit soda and salt.*

When it comes to cooky baking, Christmas is the time to shine. Attractive plates full of delicious holiday specialties and a tree brimming with attractive cooky ornaments help your home display the good cheer you feel.

Berlinerkranzer (p. 47)

Zucker Hütchen (p. 47)

Krumkake (p. 48)

Cream Wafers (p. 40)

BERLINERKRANZER

Delicious and buttery, these gay little cooky wreaths are made each holiday season in Norway. See color picture opposite.

1½ cups shortening (half butter or margarine)	4 cups all-purpose flour
1 cup sugar	1 egg white
2 tsp. grated orange rind	2 tbsp. sugar
2 eggs	red candied cherries
	green citron

Mix shortening, 1 cup sugar, rind, and eggs thoroughly. Measure flour by dipping method (p. 5) or by sifting. Stir in flour. Chill dough.

Heat oven to 400° (mod. hot). Break off small pieces of dough and roll to pencil size, about 6" long and ¼" thick. (If rich dough splits apart or seems crumbly, let it warm or work in a few drops of liquid until the dough sticks together.) Form each piece into a circle, bringing one end over and through in a single knot. Leave ½" end on each side. Place on ungreased baking sheet. Beat egg white until frothy; gradually beat in 2 tbsp. sugar; brush tops with this meringue. Press bits of red candied cherries on center of knot for holly berries. Add little jagged leaves cut out of green citron. Bake 10 to 12 min., or until set but not brown. *Makes about 6 doz. 2" cookies.*

Note: *You may use self-rising flour in this recipe.*

ZUCKER HÜTCHEN

These delightful cookies are appropriately called Little Sugar Hats. See color picture opposite.

⅓ cup butter or margarine	¼ cup finely cut-up citron
½ cup sugar	½ tsp. baking powder
1 egg yolk	Almond Meringue (below)
2 tbsp. milk	Decorator Icing (below)
1 cup plus 6 tbsp. all-purpose flour	

Cream butter and sugar until fluffy. Stir in egg yolk, then milk. Measure flour by dipping method (p. 5) or by sifting. Add citron which has been dredged in 4 tbsp. flour to butter mixture; stir in. Add 1 cup plus 2 tbsp. flour and baking powder; blend well. Chill.

Heat oven to 350° (mod.). Roll dough ⅛" thick on lightly floured board; cut out small rounds with cooky cutter (2"). Place 1" apart on a greased baking sheet. Put 1 tsp. Meringue in center of each round to make it look like the crown of a hat. Bake 10 to 12 min. When cookies are cool, pipe around crown of hat with Icing to look like a hatband. *Makes 5 doz. cookies.*

Note: *If you use self-rising flour, omit baking powder.*

Almond Meringue: Beat 1 egg white until frothy. Add 1½ cups sifted confectioners' sugar; beat until meringue holds its shape. Fold in ½ cup almonds, finely chopped.

Decorator Icing: Gradually add 1 to 2 tbsp. water to 2 to 2½ cups sifted confectioners' sugar, mixing until icing is stiff. Add 1 to 2 drops food coloring.

FATTIGMANDS BAKKELS

"Poor man's food." Scandinavian fried cookies. Dough is rolled thin for crisp texture. See color picture below.

3 egg yolks	1 tbsp. rum flavoring
1 whole egg	1 tsp. vanilla
½ tsp. salt	1 cup all-purpose
¼ cup confectioners'	flour
sugar	

Heat deep fat (at least 2″ deep) to 375°. Beat egg yolks, whole egg, and salt together until very stiff, about 10 min. Blend in confectioners' sugar and flavorings thoroughly. Measure flour by dipping method (p. 5) or by sifting. Add flour all at once; mix well. Knead dough on well-floured cloth-covered board until surface is blistered in appearance, about 7 min. Divide in half; roll out each half very thin. With pastry wheel or knife, cut dough into 4x2″ diamonds. Make 1″ slit in center of each; draw a long point of diamond through slit and curl back in opposite direction. Fry until delicately browned in deep hot fat, about ½ min. Turn quickly and brown other side. Drain on absorbent paper. Sprinkle with confectioners' sugar just before serving. *Makes 2 to 3 doz. cookies.*

Note: *If you use self-rising flour, omit salt.*

KRUMKAKE

A Scandinavian delicacy from Katherine Bergford of our staff, who usually bakes a double batch and stores them carefully in waxed paper-lined cardboard boxes for the just-before-Christmas enjoyment of all her grandchildren. See color picture, p. 46.

4 eggs	1 tsp. vanilla
1 cup sugar	¾ cup all-purpose
½ cup butter or	flour
margarine, melted	2 tsp. cornstarch
5 tbsp. cream	

Heat krumkake iron over small electric or plain gas surface unit (6″) on med. high heat. Beat eggs and sugar together thoroughly; add butter, cream, and vanilla. Measure flour by dipping method (p. 5) or by sifting. Blend flour and cornstarch; stir into egg mixture. Beat until smooth. Test iron with a few drops of water; if they "jump," iron is correct temperature. Drop batter (about ½ tbsp. for 6″ iron, more for larger irons) on ungreased iron; close gently—do not squeeze. Bake on each side about 15 seconds, or until light, golden brown. Keep iron over heat at all times. (Do not be alarmed if first few are dark; iron cools slightly while in use.) Remove with knife; immediately roll on wooden roller. *Makes 6 to 7 doz. 4″ krumkake.*

Note: *You may use self-rising flour in this recipe.*

MARZIPAN COOKIES

Exciting little cookies adapted from the attractive and expensive candy called marzipan.

½ cup butter or margarine
¼ cup sugar
food coloring (see right for amount and color)
⅛ tsp. almond flavoring
1¼ cups all-purpose flour

Cream butter, sugar, food coloring, and flavoring. Measure flour by dipping method (p. 5) or by sifting. Stir in flour; mix thoroughly. Shape as directed (right). For most cookies, use 2 level tsp. dough to form cookies. Place cookies on ungreased baking sheet. Chill 30 min.

Heat oven to 300° (slow). Bake about 30 min. (depending on size and thickness of cooky), or until done but not brown. *Makes 2 to 2½ doz. cookies.*

Note: *Do not use self-rising flour in this recipe.*

ORANGE DOUGH

Use 3 drops red food coloring and 2 drops yellow food coloring.

Oranges: Form into round ball. Insert clove in blossom end. For rough skin, punch cooky with blunt end of toothpick.

Apricots: Roll dough into ball. Make crease down one side with toothpick. Stick clove in blossom end. Use red blush (see pears).

YELLOW DOUGH

Use 2 to 3 drops yellow food coloring.

Bananas: Roll dough into banana shape, tapering ends. Flatten top slightly to show planes on fruit and curve slightly. Paint on characteristic markings with mixture of 3 drops red, 2 drops yellow, and 1 drop blue food coloring diluted in ½ tsp. water.

Pears: Roll dough into ball; then into cone shape. Bend top slightly. Insert piece of cinnamon stick for stem. For red blush, dilute ⅛ tsp. red food coloring with 1 tsp. water; paint cheeks.

RED DOUGH

Use 4 to 5 drops red food coloring.

Apples: Roll dough into ball. Stick small piece of cinnamon stick in stem top and clove in blossom end. Use red blush (see pears).

Strawberries: Roll dough into ball; form in heart shape. Cooky should be about ¾" high. For texture, punch cooky with blunt end of toothpick. Roll in red decorators' sugar, if desired. Place small piece of green-colored toothpick or green dough in top for stem.

GREEN DOUGH

Use 4 to 5 drops green food coloring.

Green Peas: Form dough in flat 1½ to 2" circle. Divide 1 level tsp. dough in 3 to 4 equal parts; form peas. Place in center of round; shape dough up and around peas. Pinch ends of pod together.

Green Apples: Shape as red apples (above).

CHRISTMAS COOKY
GIFT CONTAINERS

Coffee Cans: Cover cans with gay Christmas gift wrap, gluing it to the can and lid with all-purpose glue. For a 1-lb. can, you will need a circle 4" in diameter for lid top and a strip of paper 5¼" wide and 12½" long to glue around can.

Another attractive way to decorate coffee cans is spray painting. Easy-to-use aerosol cans of paint are available in a wide variety of colors—and the paint dries in seconds. You could spray the can red or green, then letter "Merry Christmas" with gold ink and a small paint brush. For a gift can that could be used to store cookies the year round, choose a color that will harmonize with your friend's kitchen, adding a holiday touch with ribbons and a pine cone.

Rolled Oats or Corn Meal Boxes: Adhesive-backed paper is handy for covering boxes like these. After covering, decorate with rickrack, lace edging, or designs cut from last year's Christmas cards—all glued in place.

Beautiful four-color holiday photographs cut from women's magazines make unusual coverings, too.

Plastic Freezer Boxes: Plastic containers for refrigerator or freezer use make perfect gift containers for cookies. You can bake cookies and fill boxes, then store in freezer; only the gift wrapping is left for the busy pre-holiday days.

Apothecary Jars: For your prettiest, most colorful cookies, use apothecary jars (inexpensive copies of the famous old containers used in apothecary shops). You may want to trim the jar with gold braid or tiny shells glued in designs. Or pack the cooky-filled jar in a box and gift-wrap the box.

Russian
Teacakes
(p. 25)

Holiday
Fruit Drops
(p. 146)

Chocolate
Crinkles
(p. 23)

Butter Crunch
Confection-Cookies
(p. 134)

Kaleidoscope
Cookies
(p. 127)

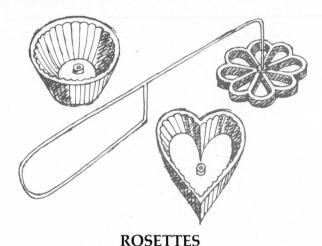

ROSETTES

Perfect rosettes are crisp yet tender.

½ cup all-purpose flour	½ cup water or milk
1 tbsp. sugar	1 egg, slightly beaten
½ tsp. salt	1 tbsp. vegetable oil
	confectioners' sugar

Measure flour by dipping method (p. 5) or by sifting. Blend dry ingredients together. Mix remaining ingredients; stir in. Strain mixture. Heat rosette iron in hot fat (400°) 3" deep in small saucepan. Tap off excess fat on absorbent paper. Dip into batter until ⅔ covered. Immerse in hot fat. Fry until delicately browned. Remove; tip upside-down to drain. Push off rosette.

Heat iron in fat again; repeat process. If iron is too cool, batter will slip off into fat; if iron is too hot, batter will stick. Stir batter each time before dipping in iron. Sprinkle rosettes with confectioners' sugar. (Best if made only a day or two before served.) Store rosettes in single layers in waxed paper-lined boxes. *Makes 18 rosettes.*

Note: *If you use self-rising flour, omit salt.*

BUTTERY NUT ROUNDS

Heat oven to 350° (mod.). Make dough for Russian Teacakes (p. 25). Roll dough about ¼" thick (rather less than more) on lightly floured cloth-covered board. Cut with cooky cutter 1½" in diameter. Place on ungreased baking sheet. Bake 10 to 12 min., or until set but not browned. Cool. Sprinkle with confectioners' sugar, frost with a bitter chocolate icing, or stack together with raspberry jam. *Makes 8 doz. cookies.*

LEBKUCHEN

Traditional Christmas honey cakes from the Black Forest region of Germany.

½ cup honey	½ tsp. soda
½ cup molasses	1 tsp. cinnamon
¾ cup brown sugar (packed)	1 tsp. cloves
	1 tsp. allspice
1 egg	1 tsp. nutmeg
1 tbsp. lemon juice	⅓ cup cut-up citron
1 tsp. grated lemon rind	⅓ cup chopped nuts
2¾ cups all-purpose flour	Glazing Icing (below)

Mix honey and molasses; bring to a boil. Cool thoroughly. Stir in sugar, egg, lemon juice, and rind. Measure flour by dipping method (p. 5) or by sifting. Stir dry ingredients together; blend in. Mix in citron and nuts. Chill dough overnight.

Heat oven to 400° (mod. hot). Roll small amount of dough at a time, keeping rest chilled. Roll out ¼" thick on lightly floured board; cut in oblongs, 2½x 1½". Place 1" apart on greased baking sheet. Bake 10 to 12 min., or until no imprint remains when touched lightly. Brush Icing lightly over cookies immediately. Quickly remove from baking sheet. Cool and store in airtight container with cut orange or apple for a few days to mellow. *Makes 6 doz. cookies.*

Note: *Do not use self-rising flour in this recipe.*

Glazing Icing: Blend 1 cup sugar and ½ cup water in small saucepan. Boil until first indication of thread appears (230° on candy thermometer). Remove from heat. Stir in ¼ cup confectioners' sugar. If icing becomes sugary while brushing cookies, reheat slightly, adding a little water until clear again. Any leftover icing may be used on fruitcake or other fruit bars.

SPRINGERLE

Specially carved boards or rolling pins used for stamping the designs on these hard anise-flavored cookies were brought to our country by German families.

2 eggs
1 cup sugar

2¼ cups all-purpose
**   flour**
anise seed

Beat eggs and sugar together thoroughly. Measure flour by dipping method (p. 5) or by sifting. Stir in flour until dough is well blended and very stiff. Refrigerate the dough for 3 to 4 hr. Roll out dough about ⅛" thick on lightly floured board. Press well-floured *springerle* board or rolling pin down firmly on dough to emboss the designs. Cut out the little squares; let dry on lightly floured board sprinkled with anise for at least 10 hr. at room temperature.

Heat oven to 325° (slow mod.). Transfer to ungreased baking sheet. Bake 12 to 15 min. *Makes about 8 doz. cookies.*

Note: *Do not use self-rising flour in this recipe.*

KRINGLA

From Norway . . . Kringla brings happy memories of childhood to Jeannette Korslund, Ames, Iowa.

1½ cups sugar
1 egg, beaten
2½ cups commercial
**   sour cream**

4 cups all-purpose
**   flour**
2 tsp. soda
¼ tsp. salt

Heat oven to 350° (mod.). Mix sugar, egg, and cream. Measure flour by dipping method (p. 5) or by sifting. Mix flour, soda, and salt; blend thoroughly into cream mixture. Divide dough in half; form each half into a long roll. If kitchen is warm, refrigerate one roll until ready to use. Cut off a narrow slice of dough. Roll lightly with hands on lightly floured board into pencil-like strip 7 to 8" long. Form a modified figure 8 by pinching ends together tightly; bring pinched ends to center of the ring; tuck under, fastening securely. Place on lightly greased baking sheet. Repeat with remaining dough. Bake 12 to 15 min., or until lightly golden. *Makes 6 to 7 doz. cookies.*

Note: *If you use self-rising flour, omit soda and salt.*

GERMAN SPICE CAKES

Traditional in German households. They have a hard texture and are good "dunking" cookies.

¾ cup sugar
¾ cup honey
2 eggs
3½ cups all-purpose
**   flour**
1 tsp. baking powder
1 tsp. cinnamon
⅛ tsp. allspice

1 cup chopped
**   almonds**
¾ cup chopped
**   candied orange**
**   peel**
Egg White Icing
**   (below)**

Heat oven to 400° (mod. hot). Mix sugar, honey, and eggs thoroughly. Measure flour by dipping method (p. 5) or by sifting. Blend dry ingredients; stir into sugar mixture. Mix in almonds and orange peel. Roll ¼" thick on lightly floured board; cut in fancy shapes. Place on lightly greased baking sheet, leaving ½" between cookies. Brush cookies with Icing. Bake 10 to 12 min. Store cookies in covered container for 1 week to mellow. *Makes about 4 doz. cakes.*

Note: *If you use self-rising flour, omit baking powder.*

Egg White Icing: Blend ½ cup confectioners' sugar, 1 egg white, and ½ tsp. lemon juice. Beat with electric or rotary beater for 5 min.

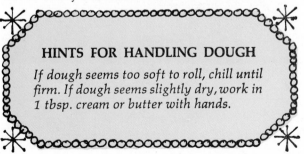

HINTS FOR HANDLING DOUGH

If dough seems too soft to roll, chill until firm. If dough seems slightly dry, work in 1 tbsp. cream or butter with hands.

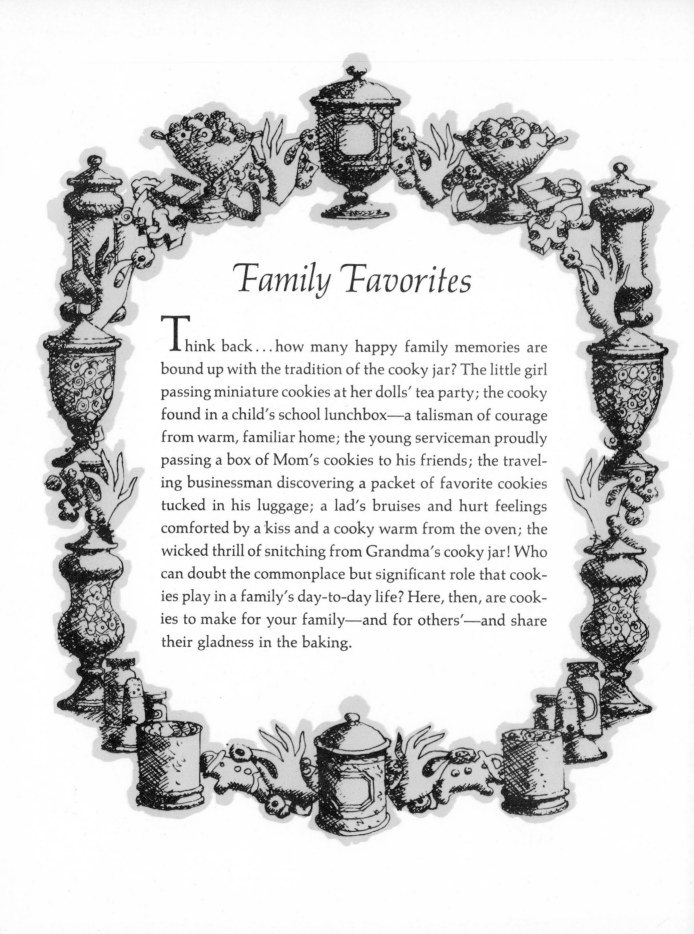

Family Favorites

Think back...how many happy family memories are bound up with the tradition of the cooky jar? The little girl passing miniature cookies at her dolls' tea party; the cooky found in a child's school lunchbox—a talisman of courage from warm, familiar home; the young serviceman proudly passing a box of Mom's cookies to his friends; the traveling businessman discovering a packet of favorite cookies tucked in his luggage; a lad's bruises and hurt feelings comforted by a kiss and a cooky warm from the oven; the wicked thrill of snitching from Grandma's cooky jar! Who can doubt the commonplace but significant role that cookies play in a family's day-to-day life? Here, then, are cookies to make for your family—and for others'—and share their gladness in the baking.

Children love cookies. And mothers—not to mention grandmothers, friends, and neighbors—love to bake cookies for children. Here are Storybook Cookies to bake and enjoy while retelling childhood's favorite tales. Nutritious and delicious cookies for growing youngsters are included, of course, though every chapter of this book has cookies children love. You'll also find complete directions for a Cooky House constructed of packaged cookies—a perfect party centerpiece.

MONKEY-FACED COOKIES

Children can hardly wait until these cookies are out of the oven to see the comical expressions that the raisin faces have taken on in baking.

½ cup shortening
1 cup brown sugar
   (packed)
½ cup molasses
½ cup milk
1 tsp. vinegar

2½ cups all-purpose
   flour
1 tsp. soda
½ tsp. salt
½ tsp. ginger
½ tsp. cinnamon
   raisins

Heat oven to 375° (quick mod.). Mix shortening, sugar, and molasses thoroughly. Mix milk and vinegar; stir in. Measure flour by dipping method (p. 5) or by sifting. Stir dry ingredients together; blend into sugar mixture. Drop rounded teaspoonfuls of dough 2½" apart on ungreased baking sheet. Place 3 raisins on each for eyes and mouth. Bake 10 to 12 min., or until set. Allow to remain on baking sheet 1 min. before removing. The faces take on droll expressions in baking. *Makes about 4 doz. 2½" cookies.*

Note: *If you use self-rising flour, omit salt and reduce soda to ¼ tsp.*

MALTED MILK ROUNDS

4 cups all-purpose
   flour
¾ cup malted milk
   powder (plain)
2 tsp. baking powder
½ tsp. soda
½ tsp. salt
1 cup butter or
   margarine

2 cups brown sugar
   (packed)
2 eggs
⅓ cup commercial
   sour cream
2 tsp. vanilla
Malt Frosting (below)

Measure flour by dipping method (p. 5) or by sifting. Blend first five ingredients thoroughly. Cream butter; gradually add sugar. Blend in eggs; beat well. Add half the blended dry ingredients; mix thoroughly. Add sour cream and vanilla; stir in remaining dry ingredients. Chill at least 4 hr.

Heat oven to 375° (quick mod.). Divide dough and roll ¼" thick on well-floured pastry cloth. Cut with 2½" cutter. Bake 12 to 15 min. on ungreased baking sheet. Cool about 2 min. Remove to racks. Cool; frost tops with Frosting. *Makes about 5 doz. cookies.*

Note: *If you use self-rising flour, omit soda and salt.*

Malt Frosting

½ cup brown sugar
   (packed)
¼ cup butter or
   margarine
¼ cup milk or cream

⅓ cup malted milk
   powder (plain)
½ tsp. vanilla
3 cups sifted
   confectioners'
   sugar

Cook brown sugar, butter, and milk in saucepan until sugar is melted. Remove from heat; stir in malted milk powder and vanilla. Blend in confectioners' sugar gradually until of right consistency.

STORYBOOK COOKIES

Almost every beloved children's story includes an animal, fruit, or other motif that could be used for a storybook cooky. Try those suggested on these pages or work out your own. For example, a crown shape trimmed with gumdrop and silver dragée "jewels" for stories of kings and princesses. Or a boot cooky cutter might be used for Puss in Boots or Long John Silver's Boots. See color picture opposite.

Peter Rabbits: Make dough for Ethel's Sugar Cookies (p. 18). Cut out cookies using rabbit cooky cutter.

Peter Rabbit's Carrots: Make Orange Dough for Marzipan Cookies (p. 49). Shape carrots by rolling 2 tsp. dough into 2″ roll; taper at ends. If you wish to add a stem, use a bit of green-colored toothpick.

Ugly Ducklings: Prepare your favorite dough for rolled cookies, such as Mary's Sugar Cookies (p. 18). Cut with duck cutter. Frost and decorate as desired.

Black Beauty: Use horse cooky cutter with favorite rolled cooky dough. Frost with Marie's Chocolate Icing (p. 150).

Children love imaginatively shaped cookies! Design your own cooky cutters or use any of the patterns on p. 103.

Trace pattern and paste on cardboard; cut out. When using, grease back, lay on rolled dough; cut around pattern with knife.

Storybook Cookies (this page)

Gingham Dogs and Calico Cats (this page)

GINGHAM DOGS AND CALICO CATS

"Everyone knows of the terrible spat of the gingham dog and the calico cat." See color picture opposite.

Make dough for Mary's Sugar Cookies (p. 18). Chill 2 to 3 hr. Heat oven to 375° (quick mod.).

Dogs: Roll half of dough ⅛ to ¼″ thick on well-floured board. Cut cookies around pattern (trace on tissue paper, then on cardboard) or use dog cutter. Place on greased baking sheet. Paint gingham design with Egg Yolk Paint (below). (Or bake first, decorate with colored icing in gingham designs.) Bake 6 to 8 min. *Makes 2 doz. dogs.*

Cats: Roll other half of dough. Cut cookies using cat pattern or use cat cutter. Place on greased baking sheet. Paint calico designs with Egg Yolk Paint (below). Bake 6 to 8 min. *Makes 3 doz. cats.*

HINT

If desired, bits of colored dough may be rolled into white dough before cutting cats; omit painting.

PAINTBRUSH COOKIES

There is a bit of the artist in every child and painting cookies is just as much fun as painting and coloring on paper.

Make dough for Ethel's Sugar Cookies (p. 18) or Merry Christmas Cookies (p. 31). Roll out. Cut a dozen cookies at a time, so unbaked cookies won't dry out before they are painted.

Place cookies on greased baking sheet. Prepare Egg Yolk Paint (below). Paint designs on cookies—use your imagination—be creative! Bake cookies as recipe directs. For clear colors, do not let cookies brown.

Egg Yolk Paint: Blend well 1 egg yolk and ¼ tsp. water. Divide mixture among several small custard cups. Add a different food coloring to each cup to make bright colors. Paint designs on cookies with small paintbrushes. If paint thickens on standing, add a few drops of water.

PICTURE BLOCK COOKIES

An idea for a child's party. The base of the cooky block is made of plain cooky dough but decorated with one of the suggested ideas before baking. Children may decorate the cookies themselves.

Make dough for Ethel's Sugar Cookies (p. 18). Chill ¾ of dough about 1 hr. Divide remaining ¼ of dough in 3 parts. Tint one part green, one yellow, and one red with a few drops of food coloring. Shape (see below). If desired, instead of tinting dough you may paint designs on blocks with food coloring or Egg Yolk Paint (p. 57).

Heat oven to 375° (quick mod.). Roll the chilled dough ⅛" thick; cut in 3" squares or 6x3" rectangles. Place 1" apart on ungreased baking sheet. Decorate with desired shapes (below). Bake 8 to 10 min., or until delicately browned. *Makes about 3 doz. squares or 1½ doz. rectangles.*

Play School Shapes: Shape each color in 4" roll (red in cylinder shape, green in square, yellow in triangle). Freeze or chill until very firm. Slice and form designs on blocks.

Molded Shapes: Chill colored dough 1 hr. Shape numbers, letters, and other simple designs and place on cooky blocks.

MAGIC CARPET COOKIES

1 cup butter or margarine	2⅔ cups all-purpose flour
½ cup sugar	½ tsp. baking powder
1 egg	½ tsp. salt
1 tbsp. flavoring (almond or vanilla)	jelly or Thin Confectioners' Sugar Icing (p. 151)

Heat oven to 375° (quick mod.). Mix butter, sugar, egg, and flavoring until creamy. Measure flour by dipping method (p. 5) or by sifting. Mix dry ingredients; blend into butter mixture. Divide dough in half. Reserve half for trim. Roll remaining dough in two rectangles, 12x6", on well-floured cloth-covered board. Cut each rectangle lengthwise in 3 equal strips. With spatula, carefully lift each strip to an ungreased baking sheet, placing about 1" apart. Spoon reserved dough into cooky press. If dough is too dry to go through cooky press, work in 1 to 2 tsp. cream. Using smallest star design, press out in long ropes on each side of each strip and also one down the center. Bake about 10 min., or until edges are delicately browned. Cool. Fill in between the rows of "trim" with jelly or Icing. Carefully cut 1" diagonal pieces with sharp knife. *Makes 60 to 70 cookies.*

Note: *Do not use self-rising flour in this recipe.*

ALICE'S OATMEAL ROUNDS

Crunchy, sugar-topped cookies. The recipe came from Alice Totushek, whose five lively youngsters request them regularly.

1 cup sugar	½ cup raisins
1 cup shortening (half butter or margarine)	1¾ cups all-purpose flour
2 eggs	1 tsp. soda
1 tsp. vanilla	½ tsp. salt
1 cup rolled oats	½ tsp. cinnamon

Mix sugar, shortening, eggs, and vanilla thoroughly. Measure flour by dipping method (p. 5) or by sifting. Blend rest of ingredients into shortening mixture. Refrigerate 4 to 5 hr. or overnight.

Heat oven to 375° (quick mod.). Roll dough in 1" balls. Place on ungreased baking sheet. Flatten with greased bottom of glass dipped in sugar. Bake 10 min. *Makes 4½ doz. cookies.*

Note: *If you use self-rising flour, omit soda and salt.*

GOLDEN CARROT COOKIES

Mysterious flavor—moist and flavorful. Next time you cook carrots for dinner, add an extra cup for use in these cookies.

1 cup shortening (part butter or margarine)	2 tsp. baking powder
¾ cup sugar	½ tsp. salt
2 eggs	¾ cup shredded coconut
1 cup mashed cooked carrots	Orange Butter Icing (p. 150)
2 cups all-purpose flour	

Heat oven to 400° (mod. hot). Mix shortening, sugar, eggs, and carrots. Measure flour by dipping method (p. 5) or by sifting. Blend flour, baking powder, and salt into shortening mixture. Mix in coconut. Drop dough by teaspoonfuls about 2" apart on lightly greased baking sheet. Bake 8 to 10 min., or until no imprint remains when touched lightly. Frost cooled cookies with Icing. *Makes 4 doz. cookies.*

Note: *If you use self-rising flour, omit baking powder and salt.*

LOLLIPOP COOKIES

Make Mary's Sugar Cookies (p. 18)—except cut 2½ to 3" circles. Bake 7 to 8 min. in 375° (quick mod.) oven. Cool.

To make lollipop: prepare a triple recipe of Easy Creamy Icing (p. 150); spread on plain baked cooky. Place a flat wooden stick or colored plastic straw across the middle, letting one end extend beyond edge of cooky. Place another cooky on top; press down slightly. Decorate with faces of tinted icing. *Makes about 2 doz. lollipops.*

TRAFFIC LIGHT COOKIES

Make these to help the children learn that it is red for "stop" and green for "go."

Make dough for Ethel's Sugar Cookies (p. 18). Heat oven to 400° (mod. hot). Divide dough in 3 parts. Roll to ¼" thick on well-floured cloth-covered board. Cut in either 3x2" rectangles with a knife, or 3" circles with cooky cutter. Using a thimble, make three indentations in cookies. Place on ungreased baking sheet. Bake 6 to 8 min., or until very lightly browned. When cookies are browned, reinforce indentations with thimble. Place 3 to 4 tbsp. orange marmalade in each of 3 cups. Tint one red, one green; the other is already yellow. Fill indentations with colored marmalade, giving the effect of a traffic light. *Makes 2½ to 3 doz. cookies.*

CEREAL MOLASSES PATTIES

If your children like caramel corn, they'll love these crispy confections.

4 cups O-shaped   ½ cup water
   puffed oat cereal   1 tbsp. plus 1 tsp.
1½ cups salted   vinegar
   peanuts   ⅛ tsp. cream of tartar
1½ cups brown sugar   1½ tsp. soda
   (packed)
¾ cup light molasses

Measure cereal and peanuts into large greased bowl. Mix sugar, molasses, water, vinegar, and cream of tartar in saucepan. Cook over low heat, stirring occasionally, to hard ball stage (250°). (A hard ball forms when a small amount of syrup is dropped into cold water.) Remove from heat. Blend in soda; mixture becomes fluffy and porous. Pour syrup over cereal-peanut mixture. Mix well with greased spoon. Allow to cool slightly to thicken. With greased hands, form mixture in patties. Cool on a greased baking sheet or waxed paper. *Makes about 3 doz. 2" patties.*

CHERRY BLINKS

⅓ cup shortening   ¼ tsp. salt
½ cup sugar   ½ cup raisins or
1 egg   cut-up dates
1½ tbsp. milk   ½ cup nuts, chopped
½ tsp. vanilla   1½ cups whole wheat
1 cup all-purpose   flakes cereal,
   flour   crushed
½ tsp. baking powder   candied or mara-
¼ tsp. soda   schino cherries

Heat oven to 375° (quick mod.). Mix shortening, sugar, and egg. Stir in milk and vanilla. Measure flour by dipping method (p. 5) or by sifting. Blend dry ingredients together; stir in. Mix in raisins and nuts. Drop dough by teaspoonfuls into cereal. Roll gently so balls of dough are completely coated. Place about 2" apart on greased baking sheet. Top with a piece of cherry. Bake 10 to 12 min., or until no imprint remains when touched lightly. *Makes about 3 doz. cookies.*

Note: *If you use self-rising flour, omit baking powder, soda, and salt.*

FRUIT-FLAVORED PUFFS

¾ cup butter or   1½ cups all-purpose
   margarine   flour
1½ cups sugar   ½ tsp. soda
1 egg   1 tsp. salt
1 tsp. almond extract   1 cup rolled oats
¼ cup water   4 cups fruit-flavored
                             corn puffs cereal

Heat oven to 375° (quick mod.). Mix butter, sugar, egg, flavoring, and water well. Measure flour by dipping method (p. 5) or by sifting. Blend flour, soda, salt; add to the sugar mixture. Mix in rolled oats and cereal. Drop by spoonfuls on greased baking sheet. Bake 10 to 12 min. *Makes 5 doz. cookies.*

Note: *If you use self-rising flour, omit soda and salt.*

CHOCOLATE PUFF BALLS

1 cup sugar   1½ sq. unsweetened
⅓ cup water   chocolate (1½ oz.)
⅓ cup light corn syrup   1 tsp. vanilla
1 tsp. salt   8 cups chocolate-
¼ cup butter or   flavored corn
   margarine   puffs cereal

Mix sugar, water, corn syrup, salt, butter, and chocolate in saucepan. Heat until chocolate is melted. Bring to boil; cook to 250° on candy thermometer or until a few drops form a hard ball when dropped in cold water. Remove from heat. Stir in vanilla. Pour hot syrup over cereal in large buttered bowl. Stir constantly to distribute syrup. Form in balls with buttered hands. If balls pull apart, reshape occasionally until they harden. *Makes 16 large balls.*

Fruit-flavored Puffs
(this page)

Chocolate Puff Balls
(this page)

Cereal
Molasses Patties
(this page)

Cherry Blinks
(this page)

PEANUT THINS

An all-around good family cooky . . . yet attractive enough to serve to company, too.

¾ cup shortening
  (part butter or
  margarine)
1 cup brown sugar
  (packed)
¼ cup peanut butter
1 egg yolk
1 tsp. vanilla

1¾ cups all-purpose
  flour
Thin Confectioners'
  Sugar Icing
  (p. 151)
½ cup chopped salted
  peanuts

Heat oven to 350° (mod.). Mix shortening, sugar, peanut butter, egg yolk, and vanilla until light and fluffy. Measure flour by dipping method (p. 5) or by sifting. Add flour; mix thoroughly. Knead dough with hands to form a ball. Divide dough into 2 parts. With floured rolling pin, roll each part on a separate ungreased baking sheet into 12x6" strip (be sure edges aren't too thin). Bake 13 to 14 min., or until lightly browned and set. While warm, spread with Icing. Sprinkle with chopped peanuts. Cut in bars, 3x1". *Makes 4 doz. bars.*

Note: *You may use self-rising flour in this recipe.*

QUICK PEANUT THINS

Make Peanut Thins (above)—except do not divide dough. Pat evenly into ungreased jelly roll pan, 15½x 10½x1". Bake 18 min. Finish as above. *Makes 30 bars.*

CRUNCHY NUT COOKIES

1 cup granulated
  sugar
1 cup brown sugar
  (packed)
½ cup shortening
2 eggs

1 tsp. vanilla
3 cups all-purpose
  flour
1 tsp. soda
½ tsp. salt
1 cup chopped nuts

Heat oven to 375° (quick mod.). Mix thoroughly sugars, shortening, eggs, and vanilla. Measure flour by dipping method (p. 5) or by sifting. Blend flour, soda, and salt; stir in. Add nuts. Form in 1" balls. (Dough will be dry.) Place on ungreased baking sheet. Flatten with bottom of greased glass dipped in sugar. Bake 8 to 10 min. *Makes about 5 doz. cookies.*

Note: *If you use self-rising flour, omit soda and salt.*

STIR-N-DROP OATMEAL COOKIES

1 cup all-purpose
  flour
1 tsp. baking powder
½ tsp. salt
½ tsp. cinnamon
½ tsp. ginger
1 cup brown sugar
  (packed)

1 cup rolled oats
¼ cup vegetable oil
2 tbsp. milk
1 egg
¾ cup Spanish
  peanuts, if
  desired

Heat oven to 375° (quick mod.). Measure flour by dipping method (p. 5) or by sifting. Stir dry ingredients together; add sugar and rolled oats. Mix in oil, milk, and egg thoroughly. Add peanuts. Drop teaspoonfuls of dough about 2" apart on lightly greased baking sheet. Bake about 10 min. *Makes about 3 doz. cookies.*

Note: *If you use self-rising flour, omit baking powder and salt.*

BRAZILIAN NUT COOKIES

A good, not-too-sweet cooky for young children.

1 cup all-purpose flour	1 egg
½ cup sugar	¼ cup milk
2 tsp. baking powder	2 tsp. lemon juice
½ tsp. salt	1 cup chopped Brazil nuts
2 tbsp. shortening	

Heat oven to 375° (quick mod.). Measure flour by dipping method (p. 5) or by sifting. Stir dry ingredients together. Add other ingredients except nuts; mix vigorously until well blended. Stir in nuts. Drop rounded teaspoonfuls of dough about 3″ apart on lightly greased baking sheet. Bake 8 to 12 min., or until lightly browned. *Makes 2½ to 3 doz. cookies.*

Note: *If you use self-rising flour, omit baking powder and salt.*

PEANUT COOKIES

Make Brazilian Nut Cookies (above)—except use chopped salted peanuts in place of Brazil nuts.

OATSIES

A delicious caramel-like oat confection topped with chocolate.

2 cups rolled oats	½ tsp. salt
½ cup brown sugar (packed)	1 tsp. vanilla
½ cup butter or margarine	1 pkg. (6 oz.) semi-sweet chocolate pieces
¼ cup dark corn syrup	¼ cup chopped nuts

Heat oven to 400° (mod. hot). Mix oats and sugar. Melt butter; add syrup, salt, and vanilla. Pour over the oats and sugar; mix well. Pat out in greased square pan, 9x9x1¾″. Bake 8 to 10 min. Do not overbake! It will be bubbly when done. While this cools, melt chocolate. Spread on chocolate; sprinkle with nuts. Cut into bars. *Makes 32 bars.*

WHEAT FLAKES NUT DROPS

A simple stir-up-and-drop cooky. Mother may want to do the actual baking, but children can do the rest.

½ cup shortening	1 tsp. baking powder
1 cup brown sugar (packed)	½ tsp. salt
2 eggs	1 cup nuts, coarsely chopped
1 tsp. vanilla	4 cups whole wheat flakes cereal
1¼ cups all-purpose flour	

Heat oven to 375° (quick mod.). Mix shortening, sugar, eggs, and vanilla together thoroughly. Measure flour by dipping method (p. 5) or by sifting. Stir flour, baking powder, and salt together. Blend shortening and flour mixtures. Stir in nuts. Carefully fold in cereal. Drop by teaspoonfuls about 3″ apart on lightly greased baking sheet. Bake 8 to 10 min. *Makes 4 to 5 doz. cookies.*

Note: *If you use self-rising flour, omit baking powder and salt.*

PECAN CRISPS

Crisp, thin, nutty wafers with attractive glazed surface.

1½ cups all-purpose flour	1 egg, separated
1 cup sugar	3 tbsp. milk
¾ tsp. salt	1 tsp. vanilla
½ cup shortening (part butter or margarine)	1 cup pecans, finely chopped

Measure flour by dipping method (p. 5) or by sifting. Blend flour, sugar, and salt in bowl. Mix in shortening, egg yolk, milk, and vanilla thoroughly with fork. Chill dough.

Heat oven to 375° (quick mod.). Form dough in 1″ balls. Place on ungreased baking sheet. Press 1/16″ thick with bottom of greased glass dipped in sugar. Dough must be pressed very thin so cooky is wafer-like; otherwise it will be too chewy. Brush with slightly beaten egg white. Sprinkle with pecans. Bake 8 to 10 min. Do not overbake! *Makes about 5 doz. cookies.*

Note: *If you use self-rising flour, omit salt.*

COOKY HOUSE

USE THESE MATERIALS:

FOR HOUSE

Frame . . . . .1 cardboard box, at least 21x20x13''; cellophane tape or masking tape

Cement for Walls . . 3 recipes of pink Frosting ''Cement'' (p. 151); 2 recipes of yellow Frosting ''Cement'' (p. 151)

Bricks for Walls . . . 2 lb. chocolate-covered cream wafer sticks (3x½x½'')

Stones for Gable . . . 1 pkg. (1 lb.) Dutch apple cookies or vanilla cooky pops (about 1⅜'' diameter)

Shingles for Roof . . 3 pkg. (10½ oz. each) lemon thins or brown-edged wafers (about 2'' diameter)

Chimney. . . . . . . .1 small pkg. pink party mints, shaved to make one side flat

Chimney Stacks . . . 1¾'' piece peppermint stick (1'' diameter); *and* 1¼'' piece peppermint stick (½'' diameter)

Windows . . . . . . .6 scalloped rectangular tea cookies (2¼x 1½''), decorated with icing (mix ¼ cup confectioners' sugar and ¾ tsp. milk) for window panes

Shutters . . . . . . .12 pink sugar wafers, cut lengthwise to ¾'' widths

Doors . . . . .2 long fig bars (3⅝x1½''—available at soda fountains)

Door Windows . . . .8 pink party mints, shaved to make one side flat

Door Handles. . . . .2 red cinnamon candies

Light Fixtures . . . . .2 small yellow gumdrops

FOR YARD

Grass. . . . . .¾ lb. coconut, soaked in green water (colored by food coloring), then dried

Animals . . . . .chocolate animals or animal crackers coated with melted chocolate

Trees. . . . . .ice cream cones frosted with 1 recipe white Frosting ''Cement'' (p. 151) and trimmed with decorators' sugar

Path . . . . .1 small pkg. yellow party mints

Fence. . . . . .piece of cardboard (6x2'') and 1 small pkg. assorted party mints

Flowers . . . . .small round gumdrops, ring gumdrops, large square gumdrops, candy mint leaves

Flower Garden . . . .candy-coated chocolate candies

DIRECTIONS

1. Cut frame for house, roof, chimney, and chimney top from flattened cardboard box (see diagram), using a single-edged razor blade; fold up sides of house and chimney (dotted lines on diagram); tape corners in place. (If cardboard is hard to fold, lightly score outside of fold with razor blade.)

2. Place house frame (without roof) on large piece of cardboard (2 to 3 ft. sq.) which will serve as base for grass.

3. Working rapidly on one wall at a time, spread pink ''cement'' ¼'' thick. For front and back of house, firmly press bricks, door, and stones into ''cement'' (see picture opposite), supporting wall with one hand from inside. Repeat for side walls, applying bricks; omit top row to permit roof to fit properly. Put vertical corner bricks in place.

4. Attach roof by frosting a 2'' border around entire underside edge with yellow ''cement''; hold in place on top of walls for several minutes until set. Spread yellow ''cement'' ¼'' thick on one side of roof at a time. Starting with the bottom row, press top edge of shingles on ''cement.'' Each row overlaps ½ of the row beneath (see picture). Since each row of shingles is not directly over the previous row, every other row requires half a cooky at each roof edge.

5. Test chimney for fit; trim if necessary. Frost entire outside of chimney with pink ''cement''; place on roof. (Use ''cement'' at base of chimney to make it fit the roof peak, if necessary.) Press flat side of mints into ''cement'' on chimney.

6. Using pink ''cement,'' frost underside of chimney top; hold in place on chimney until set; thickly frost topside of chimney top. Press chimney stacks into ''cement.''

7. Frost underside of decorated windows thinly with leftover ''cement''; put in place. Frost long underside edge of shutter; put in place, allowing to stand out slightly.

8. Attach door handles, door windows, and light fixtures with dabs of ''cement.''

9. For fence, frost one side of the 6x2'' cardboard piece with leftover ''cement''; place mints in rows on one side, alternating colors. Repeat on other side. Frost top of fence. Set in place.

10. Decorate trees; set in place.

11. To make flowers, force small, round gumdrops into gumdrop ring. Slice mint leaves in half horizontally. Put toothpick through leaves and into bottom of small gumdrop; secure other end of toothpick in square gumdrop. Set in place.

12. Arrange flower garden, animals, and path; sprinkle grass around house.

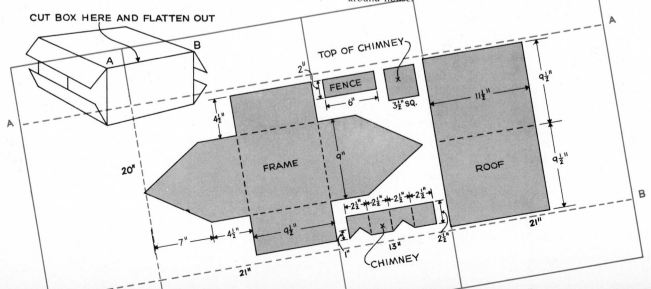

CUT BOX HERE AND FLATTEN OUT

Millions of lunches go off to school and work each day in boxes, pails, and paper bags. And many of these lunches contain cookies—to sweeten the day and provide quick energy for the afternoon ahead.

The ideal lunchbox cooky is appetizing in appearance, flavorful, and satisfying. Always pack cookies in pairs—one for lunch and one to share. Sometimes tuck in a third for an afternoon snack. And, of course, a cooky that's good in a lunchbox is just as delicious eaten for lunch or snacks at home.

NEW NORTHLAND COOKIES

½ cup shortening
(part butter or
margarine)
1 cup brown sugar
(packed)
¼ cup cold water

2 cups all-purpose
flour
1 tsp. soda
½ tsp. salt
½ tsp. cinnamon
½ cup cut-up
blanched
almonds

Mix shortening and sugar thoroughly. Stir in cold water. Measure flour by dipping method (p. 5) or by sifting. Blend dry ingredients; stir into shortening mixture. Mix in almonds. Mix thoroughly with hands. Press and mold into a long, smooth roll about 2½" in diameter. Wrap in waxed paper and chill until stiff (several hours or overnight).

Heat oven to 400° (mod. hot). Cut dough in thin slices ⅛ to 1/16" thick. Place slices a little apart on ungreased baking sheet. Bake 6 to 8 min., until lightly browned. Remove from pan immediately. *Makes about 4 doz. 2½" cookies.*

Note: *If you use self-rising flour, omit soda and salt.*

SPICED PRUNE COOKIES

Soft, yet chewy . . . made in minutes because prunes are not cooked, just cut or snipped from pits.

½ cup butter or
margarine
1 cup brown sugar
(packed)
1 egg
1¾ cups all-purpose
flour
½ tsp. soda
½ tsp. salt

½ tsp. nutmeg
½ tsp. cinnamon
⅛ tsp. ground cloves
¼ cup milk
1 cup cut-up pitted
prunes,
uncooked
½ cup chopped
walnuts

Mix butter, sugar, and egg. Measure flour by dipping method (p. 5) or by sifting. Blend flour, soda, salt, nutmeg, cinnamon, and cloves. Add to sugar mixture; blend in milk. Add prunes and walnuts, mixing well. Chill 1 hr.

Heat oven to 400° (mod. hot). Drop dough by rounded teaspoonfuls on greased baking sheet. Bake 8 to 10 min. *Makes about 4 doz. cookies.*

Note: *If you use self-rising flour, omit soda and salt.*

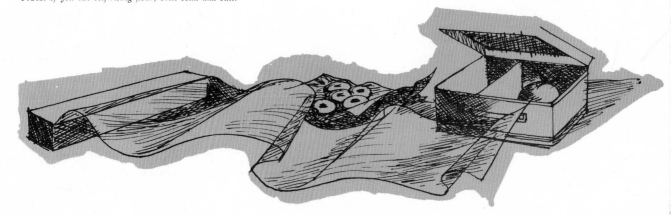

APPLESAUCE RAISIN COOKIES

¾ cup shortening	½ tsp. soda
1 cup brown sugar (packed)	½ tsp. salt
	¾ tsp. cinnamon
1 egg	¼ tsp. cloves
½ cup applesauce	1 cup raisins
2¼ cups all-purpose flour	½ cup nuts, chopped

Heat oven to 375° (quick mod.). Mix shortening, sugar, and egg thoroughly. Stir in applesauce. Measure flour by dipping method (p. 5) or by sifting. Blend dry ingredients and stir in. Mix in raisins and nuts. Drop dough by teaspoonfuls on greased baking sheet. Bake 10 to 12 min., or until lightly browned. *Makes 4 doz. cookies.*

Note: *If you use self-rising flour, omit soda and salt.*

BANANA SPICE COOKIES

¼ cup shortening	2 cups all-purpose flour
¼ cup butter or margarine	
	2 tsp. baking powder
1 cup brown sugar (packed)	¼ tsp. soda
	¼ tsp. salt
2 eggs	½ tsp. cinnamon
1 cup mashed bananas (about 2)	¼ tsp. cloves
	½ cup chopped nuts

Mix well shortening, butter, sugar, and eggs. Stir in bananas. Measure flour by dipping method (p. 5) or by sifting. Mix dry ingredients and stir in. Blend in nuts. Chill about 1 hr.

Heat oven to 375° (quick mod.). Drop rounded teaspoonfuls of dough 2″ apart on lightly greased baking sheet. Bake 8 to 10 min. If desired, frost with a thin confectioners' sugar icing. *Makes 4 doz. cookies.*

Note: *If you use self-rising flour, omit baking powder, soda, and salt.*

APPLESAUCE BROWNIES

Different; applesauce gives a nice cake-like texture.

½ cup shortening	1 cup all-purpose flour
2 sq. unsweetened chocolate (2 oz.)	
	½ tsp. baking powder
1 cup sugar	¼ tsp. soda
2 eggs, well beaten	¼ tsp. salt
½ cup applesauce	½ cup nuts, chopped
1 tsp. vanilla	

Heat oven to 350° (mod.). Melt shortening and chocolate over hot water. Blend in sugar, eggs, applesauce, and vanilla. Measure flour by dipping method (p. 5) or by sifting. Stir dry ingredients together; blend into shortening mixture. Spread batter in greased and floured square pan, 9x9x1¾″. Bake 35 to 40 min., or until top springs back when lightly touched. While hot, cut into 2¼x1½″ bars. *Makes 2 doz. bars.*

Note: *If you use self-rising flour, omit baking powder, soda, and salt.*

CEREAL COCONUT COOKIES

¼ cup shortening	1 cup all-purpose flour
½ cup brown sugar (packed)	
	½ tsp. soda
¼ cup granulated sugar	¼ tsp. salt
	1 cup coconut
1 egg	1 cup whole wheat flakes cereal
¼ tsp. vanilla	

Heat oven to 375° (quick mod.). Mix thoroughly shortening, sugars, egg, and vanilla. Measure flour by dipping method (p. 5) or by sifting. Blend dry ingredients; stir in. Blend in coconut and cereal. Drop dough by teaspoonfuls on ungreased baking sheet. Bake 8 to 10 min. *Makes 3 doz. cookies.*

Note: *If you use self-rising flour, omit soda and salt.*

COFFEE FRUIT DROPS

Chopped raw apple lends moistness to these cake-like drop cookies. The family will rave about them. See color picture opposite.

2 cups peeled and finely chopped apple	1 tsp. cinnamon
	¾ tsp. cloves
	¾ tsp. nutmeg
1 cup strong coffee or 1 tbsp. powdered instant coffee dissolved in 1 cup water	1 tsp. vanilla
	2 cups all-purpose flour
	1 tsp. soda
	¼ tsp. salt
1 cup sugar	1 cup chopped walnuts
½ cup shortening	
1 cup raisins	

Cook apple, coffee, sugar, shortening, raisins, and spices in saucepan gently until apple is tender. Remove from heat and cool.

Heat oven to 375° (quick mod.). Add vanilla to cooked mixture. Measure flour by dipping method (p. 5) or by sifting. Blend flour, soda, and salt; stir in. Mix in nuts. Drop by heaping teaspoonfuls on ungreased baking sheet. Bake about 12 min. *Makes about 6 doz. cookies.*

Note: *If you use self-rising flour, omit soda and salt.*

FIG-NUT SQUARES

Moist, rich, chewy cookies with wonderful keeping qualities. See color picture opposite.

2 eggs	½ tsp. baking powder
½ cup sugar	½ tsp. salt
½ tsp. vanilla	1½ cups finely cut-up dried figs
½ cup all-purpose flour	1 cup chopped nuts

Heat oven to 350° (mod.). Beat eggs until foamy. Beat in sugar and vanilla. Measure flour by dipping method (p. 5) or by sifting. Blend dry ingredients; mix into egg mixture. Add figs and nuts; spread in greased square pan, 9x9x1¾". Bake 25 to 30 min. *Makes 25 squares.*

DATE-NUT SQUARES

Make Fig-Nut Squares (above)—except use 2 cups finely cut-up dates in place of figs.

RAISIN CRISSCROSS COOKIES

Delicious lemon-flavored raisin cookies . . . children love them! See color picture opposite.

½ cup shortening (part butter or margarine)	1¾ cups all-purpose flour
	¾ tsp. cream of tartar
¾ cup sugar	¾ tsp. soda
1 egg	¼ tsp. salt
½ tsp. lemon extract	1 cup raisins

Heat oven to 400° (mod. hot). Mix thoroughly shortening, sugar, egg, and extract. Measure flour by dipping method (p. 5) or by sifting. Blend flour, cream of tartar, soda, and salt. Stir into shortening mixture. Mix in raisins. Roll in 1" balls. Place about 3" apart on ungreased baking sheet. Flatten with fork dipped in flour, making a crisscross pattern. Bake 8 to 10 min. *Makes about 3 doz. cookies.*

Note: *If you use self-rising flour, omit cream of tartar, soda, and salt.*

CHOCOLATE CRISSCROSS COOKIES

Make Raisin Crisscross Cookies (above)—except substitute ½ cup semi-sweet chocolate pieces for raisins.

Raisin Crisscross Cookies (this page)

Coffee Fruit Drops (this page)

Golden Nuggets (p. 72)

Fig-Nut Squares (this page)

CANADIAN HONEY DROPS

These soft brown sugar cookies look just like children's yo-yos when put together in pairs with apricot jam.

1 cup shortening (part butter or margarine)	⅓ cup honey
	1 tsp. vanilla
1 cup brown sugar (packed)	3½ cups all-purpose flour
	2 tsp. soda
2 eggs	apricot jam

Mix shortening, sugar, and eggs thoroughly. Stir in honey and vanilla. Measure flour by dipping method (p. 5) or by sifting. Blend together flour and soda; stir in. Chill until firm, several hours or overnight.

Heat oven to 350° (mod.). Roll dough in 1¼" balls. Place on ungreased baking sheet. Bake 10 to 12 min., or until almost no imprint remains when touched lightly. When slightly cooled, put together in pairs with apricot or other jam. *Makes 3 doz. double 2" cookies.*

Note: *If you use self-rising flour, omit soda.*

SUGAR 'N SPICE COOKIES

Sweetness and spice with a tenderness that's nice.

¾ cup shortening	2 tsp. soda
1 cup granulated sugar	¼ tsp. salt
	1 tsp. cinnamon
1 egg	¾ tsp. cloves
¼ cup molasses	¾ tsp. ginger
2 cups all-purpose flour	confectioners' sugar

Heat oven to 375° (quick mod.). Mix shortening, sugar, egg, and molasses thoroughly. Measure flour by dipping method (p. 5) or by sifting. Blend dry ingredients; stir into shortening mixture. Form in 1" balls. Place about 2" apart on greased baking sheet. Bake 10 to 12 min. Roll in confectioners' sugar while still warm. *Makes 4 to 5 doz. 2" cookies.*

Note: *If you use self-rising flour, reduce soda to ½ tsp. and omit salt.*

COCONUT-CHERRY COOKIES

Attractive, tender; bits of cherry and coconut give color and texture . . . from Ruth Brand.

½ cup butter or margarine	½ tsp. soda
	1½ tsp. salt
½ cup shortening	½ cup chopped candied cherries
1 cup sugar	
3 eggs	¼ cup cut-up citron
½ cup commercial sour cream	1 cup shredded coconut
3¼ cups all-purpose flour	1 tsp. grated orange rind
1 tsp. baking powder	1½ tsp. lemon or almond extract

Heat oven to 400° (mod. hot). Mix butter, shortening, sugar, and eggs thoroughly. Stir in sour cream. Measure flour by dipping method (p. 5) or by sifting. Stir dry ingredients together; blend into shortening mixture. Stir in rest of ingredients. Drop dough by rounded teaspoonfuls about 2" apart on ungreased baking sheet. Bake 10 to 12 min., or until lightly browned. *Makes 7 to 8 doz. 2" cookies.*

Note: *If you use self-rising flour, omit baking powder, soda, and salt.*

PEANUT BUTTER CRUNCHIES

A rich cooky with crisp cereal coating.

1 cup butter or margarine	1⅓ cups all-purpose flour
⅔ cup chunk-style peanut butter	½ tsp. soda
	¼ tsp. salt
1 cup brown sugar (packed)	¾ cup crushed whole wheat flakes cereal
1 egg	
1 tsp. vanilla	

Blend butter and peanut butter. Mix in sugar. Stir in egg and vanilla; beat well. Measure flour by dipping method (p. 5) or by sifting. Blend flour, soda, and salt; mix thoroughly into butter-sugar mixture. Refrigerate dough several hours, or until firm.

Heat oven to 350° (mod.). Shape dough into small balls; roll in crushed cereal. Place about 2" apart on greased baking sheet. Bake 12 to 15 min. *Makes about 4 doz. cookies.*

Note: *If you use self-rising flour, omit soda and salt.*

Cookies are such a thoughtful, personal gift to send to friends away from home, students, or men in the armed services. Here are some helpful hints to insure your cookies' fresh arrival in good condition. So bake some soon to send, with warmest wishes, to someone who is far away . . . but close to your heart.

What Cookies Travel Best?

Bar cookies, drop cookies, and fruit cookies travel well. Avoid fragile rolled cookies which may crumble before they reach their destination.

What Wrapping Materials Will Be Needed?

Use a sturdy packing box—heavier than ordinary pasteboard. Line with waxed paper. Have plenty of filler: crushed or shredded newspaper, wrapping paper, tissue paper.

Wrap Cookies Carefully.

Wrap each cooky separately in waxed paper or transparent plastic wrap. Or place cookies bottom-to-bottom in pairs and wrap each pair.

Pack Cookies in Layers.

Place a layer of filler in bottom of packing box and cover it with waxed paper. Lay wrapped cookies closely together on waxed paper. Alternate layers of cookies and filling with enough filler over the last layer of cookies to act as padding at the top. The box should be so full that you have to press down the lid to get it on. Remember to enclose a card saying who sent the box of cookies.

Wrap the Box and Address Plainly.

Wrap the box tightly with heavy paper and cord. Address plainly with permanent ink, covering the address with transparent tape or colorless nail polish. Mark the box PERISHABLE AND FRAGILE. Be sure to use the correct amount of postage.

GOLDEN CEREAL BARS

4 cups O-shaped
   puffed oat cereal
1 cup salted peanuts
1 cup coconut,
   if desired
1 cup sugar
½ cup corn syrup
1 cup cream (20%
   butterfat)

Mix cereal, peanuts, and coconut in large greased bowl. Mix sugar, corn syrup, and cream in saucepan. Cook syrup mixture over low heat, stirring occasionally, to soft ball stage (236°). (Mixture forms a soft ball when a small amount is dropped into cold water.) Remove from heat. Pour syrup mixture over cereal mixture. Mix well. Turn out into buttered square pan, 8x8x2″ or 9x9x1¾″. With hand protected by a piece of waxed paper, pat out mixture evenly in pan. Cool. Cut in bars. *Makes thirty-two 2x1″ bars.*

CHOCOLATE CHIP BARS

⅓ cup shortening
1¼ cups brown sugar
   (packed)
2 eggs
1¼ cups all-purpose
   flour
1¼ tsp. baking powder
¼ tsp. salt
½ cup semi-sweet
   chocolate pieces
   (½ of 6-oz. pkg.)
½ cup coarsely
   broken nuts

Heat oven to 350° (mod.). Mix shortening, sugar, and eggs thoroughly. Measure flour by dipping method (p. 5) or by sifting. Stir dry ingredients together and blend into shortening mixture. Stir in chocolate pieces and nuts. Spread in greased square pan, 9x9x1¾″. Bake 30 to 35 min. When almost cool, cut in bars. *Makes 16 bars.*

Note: *If you use self-rising flour, omit baking powder and salt.*

FROSTY FRUIT SQUARES

Moist, luscious, easy-to-make. Perfect for holiday gift boxes. Candied cherries, candied pineapple, or dates may be used in place of candied fruit.

⅔ cup shortening (part butter)	½ tsp. salt
1 cup sugar	½ tsp. cinnamon
1 egg	½ tsp. nutmeg
1 tbsp. grated orange rind, if desired	1 cup raisins
¼ cup orange or pineapple juice	1 cup mixed candied fruit
2½ cups all-purpose flour	½ cup chopped nuts, if desired
1 tsp. soda	Quick Cream Icing (p. 151)

Heat oven to 400° (mod. hot). Mix shortening, sugar, and egg until fluffy. Stir in rind and juice. Measure flour by dipping method (p. 5) or by sifting. Blend dry ingredients and stir into sugar mixture. Mix in fruit and nuts; pat dough evenly into greased jelly roll pan, 15½x10½x1", or into two square pans, one 8x8x 2" and one 9x9x1¾". Bake 15 to 18 min., or until top springs back when touched lightly. Cool slightly; spread on Icing. If desired, decorate with bits of candied fruit. Cut in squares. *Makes 3 doz. 2" squares.*

Note: *If you use self-rising flour, omit soda and salt.*

MORE GOOD TRAVELERS
Orange Oatmeal Cookies (p. 128)
Holiday Fruit Drops (p. 146)
Snickerdoodles (p. 23)
Mincemeat Bars (p. 129)
Chocolate Fruit Bars (p. 14)
Pecan Spice Cookies (p. 24)
Fig-Nut Squares (p. 68)

GOLDEN NUGGETS

Full of apricot nuggets. See color picture, p. 69.

1 cup dried apricots, coarsely cut up	1 tsp. vanilla
½ cup water	½ tsp. almond flavoring
1 cup shortening (part butter or margarine)	1¾ cups all-purpose flour
½ cup brown sugar (packed)	2 tsp. baking powder
½ cup granulated sugar	½ tsp. salt
1 egg	1½ to 2 cups flaked coconut
	toasted whole almonds

Cook apricots in water over low heat 5 to 10 min. (water should be absorbed). Cool. Mix shortening and sugars until fluffy. Add egg, flavorings, and apricots. Measure flour by dipping method (p. 5) or by sifting. Mix flour, baking powder, and salt; stir in. Chill dough several hours.

Heat oven to 350° (mod.). Drop heaping teaspoonfuls of dough into coconut to coat. Place 2" apart on lightly greased baking sheet. Top with an almond. Bake 12 to 15 min. *Makes 6 doz. cookies.*

Note: *If you use self-rising flour, omit baking powder and salt.*

LEMON CRINKLES

From Mrs. Alfred T. Neilsen of Council Bluffs, Iowa, who prefers simple and easy recipes that leave her time for her hobby of making hats.

½ cup shortening	1½ cups all-purpose flour
1 cup brown sugar (packed)	½ tsp. soda
1 egg	½ tsp. cream of tartar
about 1 tbsp. grated lemon rind	¼ tsp. salt
	¼ tsp. ginger
	granulated sugar

Heat oven to 350° (mod.). Mix shortening, sugar, and egg thoroughly; blend in lemon rind. Measure flour by dipping method (p. 5) or by sifting. Blend dry ingredients; stir into sugar mixture. Roll in 1" balls; dip tops in granulated sugar. Bake on ungreased baking sheet 10 to 12 min. *Makes about 3 doz. cookies.*

Note: *If you use self-rising flour, omit soda and salt.*

COCONUT LEMON BARS

2 cups all-purpose flour	½ tsp. salt
½ cup butter or margarine	1 cup finely shredded coconut
¼ cup brown sugar (packed)	½ cup raisins
3 eggs, well beaten	½ cup walnuts, chopped
2 cups brown sugar (packed)	2 tbsp. lemon juice
	1 tsp. grated lemon rind

Heat oven to 350° (mod.). Measure flour by dipping method (p. 5) or by sifting. Mix flour, butter, and ¼ cup sugar thoroughly. Press firmly into bottom of a lightly greased oblong pan, 13x9½x2″. Bake 10 min.

Mix eggs, 2 cups sugar, and salt together thoroughly. Stir in rest of ingredients. Spread evenly over the partially baked bottom layer. Bake about 25 min. Top will be lightly browned. Cut in 3x1″ bars when cool. *Makes 28 bars.*

Note: *If you use self-rising flour, omit salt.*

MONTEGO BAY SQUARES

1½ cups cut-up dates	½ cup brown sugar (packed)
2 tbsp. granulated sugar	¾ cup all-purpose flour
¾ cup water	¼ tsp. soda
½ sq. unsweetened chocolate (½ oz.)	½ tsp. salt
⅓ cup shortening (part butter or margarine)	¾ cup rolled oats
	⅓ cup chopped nuts

Heat oven to 400° (mod. hot). Grease a square pan, 8x8x2″. Cook dates, sugar, water, and chocolate over low heat, stirring constantly, until mixture thickens, about 10 min. Cool. Cream shortening and brown sugar thoroughly. Measure flour by dipping method (p. 5) or by sifting. Mix flour, soda, and salt; stir in. Mix in rolled oats and nuts. Press half of mixture over bottom of pan. Spread with date mixture; top with remaining crumbly mixture, pressing top lightly. Bake 25 to 30 min., or until golden brown. *Makes about 2 doz. bars.*

Note: *If you use self-rising flour, omit soda and salt.*

COCONUT BELLES

Since this cooky is better the second day than the day it is baked, you must bake them yesterday to enjoy them today.

½ cup shortening (part butter or margarine)	1 cup all-purpose flour
1 cup brown sugar (packed)	½ tsp. salt
1 egg	2 tsp. baking powder
½ tsp. vanilla	⅓ cup shredded coconut
¼ tsp. lemon extract	2 tbsp. finely chopped candied orange peel
2 tbsp. milk	

Heat oven to 325° (slow mod.). Mix shortening, sugar, egg, vanilla, lemon extract, and milk thoroughly. Measure flour by dipping method (p. 5) or by sifting. Mix flour, salt, and baking powder; stir in. Blend in coconut and peel. Spread in lightly greased square pan, 9x9x1¾″. Bake 30 to 35 min., or until golden brown. While warm, cut into 1½x1″ bars. Serve cool. *Makes 4 doz. bars.*

Note: *If you use self-rising flour, omit salt and baking powder.*

BANANA OATMEAL COOKIES

¾ cup shortening
1 cup sugar
1 egg, beaten
1½ cups all-purpose
flour
½ tsp. soda
1 tsp. salt
1 tsp. cinnamon
¼ tsp. nutmeg
1¾ cups rolled oats
1 cup mashed ripe
bananas (2 to 3
medium)
½ cup chopped nuts
or raisins

Heat oven to 400° (mod. hot). Measure flour by dipping method (p. 5) or by sifting. Place all ingredients in mixing bowl. Beat until well blended. Drop rounded teaspoonfuls of dough about 1½" apart on ungreased baking sheet. Bake 12 to 15 min. *Makes 4 doz. cookies.*

Note: *If you use self-rising flour, omit soda and salt.*

BANANA-CHOCOLATE CHIP COOKIES

Make Banana Oatmeal Cookies (above)—except use ½ cup chocolate pieces instead of nuts or raisins.

HIDDEN CHOCOLATE COOKIES

½ cup shortening
(part butter or
margarine)
½ cup granulated
sugar
¼ cup brown sugar
(packed)
1 egg
1 tbsp. water
½ tsp. vanilla
1⅔ cups all-purpose
flour
½ tsp. soda
¼ tsp. salt
about 2 doz. choco-
late mint wafers

Mix thoroughly shortening, sugars, and egg. Stir in water and vanilla. Measure flour by dipping method (p. 5) or by sifting. Blend flour, soda, and salt; stir in. Chill dough.

Heat oven to 400° (mod. hot). Shape cookies by enclosing each chocolate mint wafer in about 1 tbsp. dough. Place about 2" apart on ungreased baking sheet. Bake 8 to 10 min., or until no imprint remains when touched lightly. *Makes about 2 doz. cookies.*

Note: *If you use self-rising flour, omit soda and salt.*

JEWELED BARS

A chewy, moist bar with the added fun of candied orange slices. It contains no shortening but is rich in egg. "Perfect with a glass of cold milk," says Margret Johnson, who brought the recipe to us.

4 eggs, separated
2¼ cups brown sugar
(packed)
1 tbsp. water
1 tsp. vanilla
2 cups all-purpose
flour
1 tsp. baking powder
½ tsp. salt
1 cup candied orange
slices (about 18),
finely cut
¾ cup chopped
walnuts

Heat oven to 350° (mod.). Beat egg yolks; add sugar, water, and vanilla. Measure flour by dipping method (p. 5) or by sifting. Blend dry ingredients; stir in. Mix in orange pieces and walnuts. Beat egg whites until stiff but not dry; stir in. Spread in well-greased oblong pan, 13x9½x2". Bake 30 to 35 min. Cut in bars while warm. *Makes about 3 doz. bars.*

Note: *If you use self-rising flour, omit baking powder and salt.*

JEWELED GUMDROP BARS

Make Jeweled Bars (above)—except use 1 cup multi-colored gumdrops, finely cut, in place of orange slices.

FILLED MOLASSES COOKIES

½ cup shortening	½ tsp. salt
½ cup brown sugar (packed)	1 tsp. baking powder
	1 tsp. cinnamon
1 egg	¼ tsp. cloves
½ cup molasses	¼ tsp. nutmeg
¼ cup buttermilk	¾ cup orange marmalade
3 cups all-purpose flour	cut-up dates, candied fruit, or raisins
1 tsp. soda	

Heat oven to 375° (quick mod.). Mix shortening, sugar, and egg thoroughly. Stir in molasses and milk. Measure flour by dipping method (p. 5) or by sifting. Blend dry ingredients; stir in. If dough is too soft to roll, chill. Roll dough, ⅓ at a time, as thin as possible (1/16″ thick) on floured board. Cut in 2″ rounds. Place ½ tsp. marmalade on half the rounds; cover with remaining rounds. Top each cooky with a piece of cut-up date or candied fruit or a raisin. Place on lightly greased baking sheet. Bake 10 to 12 min. *Makes 5 doz. 2″ cookies.*

Note: *If you use self-rising flour, omit soda, salt, and baking powder.*

RAISIN OATMEAL DROP COOKIES

A soft, old-fashioned cooky—hearty and homey. These cookies are excellent for mailing because the mashed potatoes keep them moist and tender.

instant mashed potato puffs	1 cup all-purpose flour
1 cup brown sugar (packed)	1 tsp. salt
½ cup granulated sugar	½ tsp. soda
	1 tsp. cinnamon
¾ cup shortening	½ tsp. cloves
2 eggs	1 cup raisins
¼ cup water	1 cup chopped nuts
1 tsp. vanilla	3 cups quick-cooking rolled oats

Heat oven to 400° (mod. hot). Prepare potatoes as directed on pkg. for 2 servings (1 cup); set aside. Cream sugars, shortening, eggs, water, and vanilla until fluffy; stir in potatoes. Measure flour by dipping method (p. 5) or by sifting. Blend flour, salt, soda, and spices; stir in. Fold in raisins, nuts, and rolled oats. Drop rounded teaspoonfuls of dough on lightly greased baking sheet. Bake about 10 min. Store in container with a tight-fitting cover. *Makes 5 doz. cookies.*

Note: *If you use self-rising flour, omit salt and soda.*

CANDY-TOPPED OATMEAL BARS

1 cup butter or margarine	1 cup all-purpose flour
½ cup brown sugar (packed)	1 cup rolled oats
½ cup granulated sugar	¾ milk chocolate bar (8-oz. size)
	2 tbsp. butter
2 egg yolks	½ cup chopped nuts

Heat oven to 350° (mod.). Mix 1 cup butter, sugars, and egg yolks thoroughly. Measure flour by dipping method (p. 5) or by sifting. Stir in flour and oats. Spread in greased and floured oblong pan, 13x9½x2″. Bake 20 to 25 min. Cool 10 min. Melt chocolate and 2 tbsp. butter over hot water; spread over cooled cooky layer. Sprinkle with nuts; cut in bars. *Makes 4 doz. bars.*

Note: *You may use self-rising flour in this recipe.*

Recipes we know and use today came from 'round the world to the thirteen isolated colonies of America. Plain and hearty cookies were the gustatory pleasure of our pioneers. The homespun flavors of sour cream, maple sugar, butterscotch, and cinnamon are still among our favorites. And though our tastes may now be trained to prefer white sugar to molasses and our eyes to select a fancy frosted cooky rather than a simple oatmeal drop, these cookies of our forefathers have won an enduring place in our hearts.

JOE FROGGERS

Our adaptation of the famous molasses cookies made long ago by old Uncle Joe of Marblehead, Mass. The cookies are as plump and dark as the little frogs that lived in the pond near Joe's cottage.

½ cup shortening	1½ tsp. salt
1 cup sugar	1 tsp. soda
1 cup dark molasses	1½ tsp. ginger
½ cup water	½ tsp. cloves
4 cups all-purpose	½ tsp. nutmeg
flour	¼ tsp. allspice

Mix well shortening and sugar. Stir in molasses and water. Measure flour by dipping method (p. 5) or by sifting. Stir dry ingredients together; blend into shortening mixture. Chill dough several hours or overnight.

Heat oven to 375° (quick mod.). Roll dough ¼" thick on floured board. Cut in 3" circles. Sprinkle with sugar. Place on well-greased baking sheet. Bake 10 to 12 min. Leave on baking sheet a few min. before removing to prevent breaking. Store in covered cooky jar. *Makes 3 to 4 doz. cookies.*

Note: *If you use self-rising flour, omit salt and soda.*

ICE CREAM SANDWICHES

Slice round bulk ice cream; place slice between two Froggers (above). Or Froggers may be cut and baked as rectangles to be used with brick ice cream. After ice cream sandwiches are made, place in freezing compartment for at least an hour before serving.

SESAME SEED COOKIES

A modern-day version of early American Seed Cakes. For the original cooky, colonial mothers rolled cardamom, coriander, caraway, or sesame seeds into the rich dough.

½ cup butter or margarine	2 cups all-purpose flour
⅓ cup sesame seeds	1 tsp. baking powder
½ cup butter	¼ tsp. salt
1 cup sugar	Browned Butter
1 egg	Sesame Icing
2 tbsp. water	(below)

Heat oven to 375° (quick mod.). Brown ½ cup butter and sesame seeds in medium saucepan over low heat until golden brown (watch carefully to prevent mixture from burning); remove from heat. Mix ½ cup butter, sugar, and egg thoroughly. Add 2 tbsp. sesame seeds (from the browned butter) to sugar mixture. Blend in water.

Measure flour by dipping method (p. 5) or by sifting. Stir dry ingredients together; blend into sugar mixture. Drop dough by teaspoonfuls on ungreased baking sheet; flatten with bottom of greased glass dipped in sugar. Bake about 10 min., or until lightly browned around the edges. Cool and frost. *Makes 4 to 5 doz. cookies.*

Note: *If you use self-rising flour, omit baking powder and salt.*

Browned Butter Sesame Icing: Blend 3 cups sifted confectioners' sugar, 3 tbsp. milk, and 1 tsp. vanilla into remainder of browned butter-sesame seed mixture. Stir until smooth.

THUMBPRINT COOKIES

Nut-rich . . . the thumb dents filled with sparkling jelly. See color picture, p. 36.

½ cup shortening (part butter or margarine)	1 cup all-purpose flour
¼ cup brown sugar (packed)	¼ tsp. salt
1 egg, separated	¾ cup finely chopped nuts
½ tsp. vanilla	jelly or tinted confectioners' sugar icing

Heat oven to 350° (mod.). Mix shortening, sugar, egg yolk, and vanilla thoroughly. Measure flour by dipping method (p. 5) or by sifting. Blend together flour and salt; stir in. Roll dough into balls (1 tsp. per ball). Beat egg white slightly with fork. Dip balls in egg white. Roll in nuts. Place about 1″ apart on ungreased baking sheet; press thumb gently in center of each. Bake 10 to 12 min., or until set. Cool. Fill thumbprints with jelly or tinted icing. *Makes about 3 doz. cookies.*

Note: *If you use self-rising flour, omit salt.*

CHOCOLATE THUMBPRINT COOKIES

Make Thumbprint Cookies (above)—except substitute ½ cup granulated sugar for the brown sugar; add 1 sq. unsweetened chocolate (1 oz.), melted, with the shortening.

HARD-COOKED EGG COOKIES

1 cup butter or margarine	1 tbsp. grated lemon rind
1 cup sugar	3 cups all-purpose flour
1 egg (uncooked)	1 egg, slightly beaten
¾ cup sieved hard-cooked egg yolks (5 yolks)	blanched almonds
	2 tsp. cinnamon
	3 tbsp. sugar

Heat oven to 325° (slow mod.). Mix butter, 1 cup sugar, and raw egg thoroughly. Blend in egg yolks and rind. Measure flour by dipping method (p. 5) or by sifting. Stir in flour. Roll dough out ¼″ thick on lightly floured cloth-covered board. Cut with floured 1½″ fluted round cutter. Place on ungreased baking sheet. Brush tops of cookies with slightly beaten egg; place blanched almonds crosswise on top of each. Sprinkle with mixture of cinnamon and 3 tbsp. sugar. Bake 20 to 25 min., or until delicately browned. Store in loosely covered jar to retain crispness. *Makes about 8 doz. 1½″ cookies.*

Note: *You may use self-rising flour in this recipe.*

VERMONT MAPLE COOKIES

Vermonters flavor their cookies and cakes with maple sugar. But since it is sometimes difficult to obtain, we suggest maple flavoring for equally delicious results. See color picture, p. 78.

Make Jubilee Jumbles (p. 10)—using 1 tbsp. maple flavoring in place of vanilla. Spread cooled cookies with Maple Butter Glaze (below). *Makes 4 doz. 2½″ cookies.*

Maple Butter Glaze: Heat ½ cup butter until golden brown. Blend in 2 cups sifted confectioners' sugar and 2 tsp. maple flavoring. Stir in 2 to 4 tbsp. hot water until icing spreads smoothly.

OLD-FASHIONED SOUR CREAM COOKIES

See color picture opposite.

½ cup shortening (part butter or margarine)	1 tsp. baking powder
	½ tsp. soda
	½ tsp. salt
1 cup sugar	¼ tsp. nutmeg
1 egg	½ cup commercial
1 tsp. vanilla	sour cream
2⅔ cups all-purpose flour	

Heat oven to 425° (hot). Mix shortening, sugar, egg, and vanilla thoroughly. Measure flour by dipping method (p. 5) or by sifting. Blend dry ingredients; add to sugar mixture alternately with sour cream. Divide dough; roll out to ¼" thick on well-floured pastry cloth. Cut with 2" cutter; place on greased baking sheet. Sprinkle with sugar. Bake 8 to 10 min., or until lightly browned. *Makes 4 to 5 doz. 2" cookies.*

Note: *If you use self-rising flour, omit baking powder, soda, and salt.*

Gingerbread Boys (this page)

Old-fashioned Sour Cream Cookies (this page)

Plantation Fruit Bars (this page)

Vermont Maple Cookies (p. 77)

PLANTATION FRUIT BARS

See color picture opposite.

¼ cup shortening	1½ tsp. baking powder
½ cup sugar	
1 egg	½ tsp. salt
½ cup molasses	¼ tsp. soda
½ cup milk	1½ cups raisins or cut-up dates
2 cups all-purpose flour	1 cup chopped nuts
	Lemon Glaze (below)

Heat oven to 350° (mod.). Mix shortening, sugar, egg, and molasses thoroughly. Stir in milk. Measure flour by dipping method (p. 5) or by sifting. Blend dry ingredients; add to milk mixture. Stir in raisins and nuts. Spread in greased oblong pan, 13x9½x2". Bake 25 to 30 min., or until toothpick stuck in center comes out clean. When cool, spread with Glaze. Cut in bars. *Makes 4 doz. 2x1" bars.*

Note: *If you use self-rising flour, omit baking powder and salt.*

Lemon Glaze: Melt ⅓ cup butter. Blend in 2 cups confectioners' sugar and ½ teaspoon grated lemon peel. Stir in 2 to 4 tbsp. lemon juice until icing spreads smoothly.

GINGERBREAD BOYS

Fat, puffy cookies. See color picture opposite.

⅓ cup shortening	2 tsp. soda
1 cup brown sugar (packed)	1 tsp. salt
	1 tsp. allspice
1½ cups dark molasses	1 tsp. ginger
	1 tsp. cloves
⅔ cup cold water	1 tsp. cinnamon
7 cups all-purpose flour	Easy Creamy Icing (p. 150)

Mix shortening, sugar, and molasses thoroughly. Stir in water. Measure flour by dipping method (p. 5) or by sifting. Blend all dry ingredients; stir in. Chill.

Heat oven to 350° (mod.). Roll dough ¼" thick on lightly floured board. Cut with gingerbread boy cutter or other favorite shaped cutter. Place far apart on lightly greased baking sheet. Bake 10 to 12 min., or until no imprint remains when touched lightly. Ice cooled cookies. *Makes 2½ doz. 2½" cookies.*

Note: *If you use self-rising flour, omit soda and salt.*

JAN HAGEL

From Holland come these crisp, buttery-rich strips with baked-on nut glaze. Quick and easy, especially nice for teas or as an accompaniment to ice cream desserts. We call them Dutch Hail. See color picture opposite.

1 cup butter or margarine	½ tsp. cinnamon
1 cup sugar	1 tbsp. water
1 egg, separated	½ cup very finely chopped walnuts
2 cups all-purpose flour	

Heat oven to 350° (mod.). Lightly grease a jelly roll pan, 15½x10½x1″. Mix butter, sugar, and egg yolk. Measure flour by dipping method (p. 5) or by sifting. Blend flour and cinnamon; stir into butter mixture. Pat into pan. Beat water and egg white until frothy; brush over dough; sprinkle with nuts. Bake 20 to 25 min., or until very lightly browned. Cut immediately into finger-like strips. *Makes fifty 3x1″ strips.*

Note: *You may use self-rising flour in this recipe.*

BUTTERSCOTCH LACE COOKIES

See color picture opposite.

1 cup butter or margarine, melted	1 tbsp. molasses, if desired
1½ cups brown sugar (packed)	3 tbsp. flour
2¼ cups rolled oats	1 egg, slightly beaten
½ tsp. salt	1 tsp. vanilla

Add sugar to butter; pour over rolled oats. Let stand at room temperature overnight so oats absorb butter.

Heat oven to 375° (quick mod.). Mix remaining ingredients into oats. Drop level teaspoonfuls of dough 2″ apart on heavily greased baking sheet. Bake only 12 cookies on a sheet. Bake 5 to 7 min., or until brown around edges. Allow to remain on sheet a few min. until firm, then immediately remove with spatula to cooling rack. *Makes 6 doz. cookies.*

Note: *Do not make these cookies in hot, humid weather, as cookies absorb moisture from air and become limp.*

FILLED OATMEAL COOKIES

See color picture opposite.

2 cups all-purpose flour	1 egg
1 tsp. salt	¼ cup molasses
½ tsp. soda	1 cup rolled oats
½ cup brown sugar (packed)	Pumpkin Filling or Date Filling (below)
¾ cup shortening	

Heat oven to 375° (quick mod.). Measure flour by dipping method (p. 5) or by sifting. Blend flour, salt, and soda. Add sugar, shortening, egg, and molasses; stir until smooth. Blend in rolled oats. Roll dough out ⅛″ thick on lightly floured board. Cut with 2½″ round cutter. Place half the rounds on ungreased baking sheet. Spread 1 tsp. Filling lightly on center of each cooky. Cut a cross or other pattern on remaining rounds; place over filling-topped rounds. Seal edges. Bake 12 to 15 min. *Makes 2 doz. filled cookies.*

Note: *If you use self-rising flour, omit salt and soda.*

Pumpkin Filling: Mix 1 cup cooked or canned pumpkin, ½ cup sugar, ½ tsp. cinnamon, ½ tsp. ginger, and ¼ tsp. nutmeg.

Date Filling: Boil together 1 cup cut-up pitted dates (about ½ lb.), ½ cup sugar, and ¼ cup water until thick, stirring constantly. Stir in ½ cup chopped nuts. Cool before using.

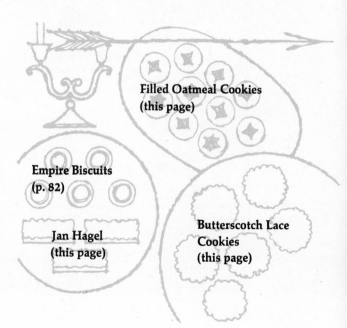

Filled Oatmeal Cookies (this page)

Empire Biscuits (p. 82)

Jan Hagel (this page)

Butterscotch Lace Cookies (this page)

EMPIRE BISCUITS

Our easy-to-make version of a cooky popular in Williamsburg, Virginia, during the golden era when that lovely city was the social center of the Southern colonies. See color picture, p. 81.

Make dough for Vanilla Refrigerator Cookies (p. 16). Shape rolls 1½" in diameter; slice thin and bake. Put two cooled cookies together with currant jelly as filling. Frost top cooky with Easy Creamy Icing (p. 150); decorate as desired.

CENTENNIAL MOLASSES SPICE DROPS

One hundred years ago homemakers used vinegar in much of their cooking—even in cooky baking.

⅔ cup shortening (part butter or margarine)	3 cups all-purpose flour
⅔ cup sugar	¾ tsp. soda
2 eggs	¼ tsp. salt
⅔ cup molasses	¾ tsp. cinnamon
	¾ tsp. ginger
	¼ cup cider vinegar

Heat oven to 375° (quick mod.). Mix shortening, sugar, eggs, and molasses thoroughly. Measure flour by dipping method (p. 5) or by sifting. Blend dry ingredients; add alternately with vinegar to batter. Mix well. Drop dough by teaspoonfuls about 2" apart on lightly greased baking sheet. Bake 8 to 10 min., or until no imprint remains when touched lightly. *Makes 5 doz. cookies.*

Note: *If you use self-rising flour, omit soda and salt.*

STONE JAR MOLASSES COOKIES

Crisp and brown . . . and so delicious.

1 cup light molasses	1¾ tsp. baking powder
½ cup shortening	
1 tsp. soda	1 tsp. salt
2¼ cups all-purpose flour	1½ tsp. ginger

Heat molasses to boiling point. Remove from heat. Stir in shortening and soda. Measure flour by dipping method (p. 5) or by sifting. Blend remaining ingredients together; stir in. Chill dough.

Heat oven to 350° (mod.). Roll dough out very thin (1/16") on lightly floured board. Cut in desired shapes. Place on lightly greased baking sheet. Bake 5 to 7 min., or until set. Do not overbake! *Makes about 6 doz. 2½" cookies.*

Note: *If you use self-rising flour, omit soda, baking powder, and salt.*

OTHER POPULAR COOKIES OF YEARS GONE BY

Cinnamon Jumbles (p. 139)
Applesauce Raisin Cookies (p. 67)
Filled Cookies (p. 19)
Filled Molasses Cookies (p. 75)
Scotch Shortbread (p. 20)
Raisin Oatmeal Drop Cookies (p. 75)
Moravian Ginger Cookies (p. 20)

CHEWY MOLASSES COOKIES

A flat wafer-like cooky.

⅓ cup shortening	½ tsp. salt
½ cup sugar	½ tsp. cinnamon
2 eggs	¼ tsp. cloves
½ cup molasses	¼ tsp. allspice
2 tbsp. milk	1 cup currants
1¼ cups all-purpose flour	½ cup chopped nuts
1 tsp. soda	2 tsp. vanilla

Cream shortening and sugar thoroughly. Stir in eggs, molasses, and milk; blend well. Measure flour by dipping method (p. 5) or by sifting. Blend dry ingredients; stir in. Add currants, nuts, and vanilla. Mix well. Chill several hours or until firm.

Heat oven to 350° (mod.). Drop dough by small teaspoonfuls about 2″ apart on well-greased baking sheet. Bake about 15 min. Let baked cookies remain on baking sheet for a moment before removing. *Makes about 4 doz. 2½″ cookies.*

Note: *If you use self-rising flour, omit soda and salt.*

HOW TO FRESHEN DROP COOKIES

Freshen drop cookies by reheating in a covered casserole in slow oven (300°) 8 to 10 min.; re-crisp cookies on an ungreased baking sheet or in a shallow pan in a slow oven (300°) 3 to 5 min.

BUTTERMILK COOKIES

½ cup shortening (part butter or margarine)	3 cups all-purpose flour
1 cup sugar	1 tsp. baking powder
1 egg	½ tsp. soda
½ cup buttermilk	½ tsp. salt
2 tsp. vanilla	1 tsp. nutmeg
	¼ cup sugar
	1 tsp. cinnamon

Mix shortening, 1 cup sugar, and egg thoroughly. Stir in buttermilk and vanilla. Measure flour by dipping method (p. 5) or by sifting. Blend dry ingredients into shortening mixture. Chill dough 1 hr.

Heat oven to 400° (mod. hot). Drop by tablespoonfuls on greased baking sheet. Flatten with bottom of greased glass dipped in mixture of ¼ cup sugar and cinnamon. Bake 8 to 10 min. *Makes about 30 cookies.*

Note: *If you use self-rising flour, omit baking powder, soda, and salt.*

SOUR CREAM-NUT COOKIES

Flavor of Grandma's sour cream rolled cookies with modern easy method of drop-and-flatten.

⅓ cup shortening	½ tsp. nutmeg
⅔ cup sugar	½ cup commercial sour cream
1 egg	
1⅔ cups all-purpose flour	½ cup finely chopped nuts
1 tsp. baking powder	1 tbsp. sugar
¼ tsp. soda	¼ tsp. nutmeg
½ tsp. salt	

Heat oven to 400° (mod. hot). Mix shortening, ⅔ cup sugar, and egg thoroughly. Measure flour by dipping method (p. 5) or by sifting. Stir dry ingredients together; blend into shortening-sugar mixture alternately with sour cream. Stir in nuts. Drop dough by teaspoonfuls about 2″ apart on greased baking sheet. Flatten with greased bottom of glass dipped in sugar. Mix 1 tbsp. sugar and nutmeg; sprinkle on top of cookies. Bake 8 to 10 min. *Makes about 3 doz. cookies.*

Note: *If you use self-rising flour, omit baking powder, soda, and salt.*

CANADIAN OATMEAL SHORTBREAD

The flavor of this delicious cooky is even better after it has been stored a few days. See color picture, p. 122.

1 cup butter or margarine	1 cup all-purpose flour
½ cup brown sugar (packed)	½ tsp. soda
1 tsp. vanilla	2 cups rolled oats

Mix butter, sugar, and vanilla until fluffy. Measure flour by dipping method (p. 5) or by sifting. Blend flour, soda, and rolled oats; stir into butter mixture. Chill 1 to 2 hr.

Heat oven to 350° (mod.). Roll dough ¼" thick on lightly floured board. Cut in 1½" squares or fancy shapes. Bake on ungreased baking sheet 10 to 12 min. *Makes 3½ to 4 doz. cookies.*

Note: *Do not use self-rising flour in this recipe.*

BUTTERSCOTCH SHORTBREAD

1 cup shortening (part butter or margarine)	¼ cup granulated sugar
½ cup brown sugar (packed)	2¼ cups all-purpose flour
	1 tsp. salt

Heat oven to 300° (slow). Mix shortening and sugars thoroughly. Measure flour by dipping method (p. 5) or by sifting. Mix flour and salt; stir in. Mix thoroughly. Roll out ¼" thick on floured cloth-covered board. Cut in desired shapes. Place on ungreased baking sheet. Bake 20 to 25 min. *Makes about 7½ doz. small cookies.*

Note: *Do not use self-rising flour in this recipe.*

ESSIE'S COOKIES

Crisp, crunchy, good-eating cooky.

½ cup butter or margarine	2 tsp. baking powder
1 cup sugar	1 egg white
1 egg	¼ cup sugar
½ tsp. almond extract	1 tsp. cinnamon
1¾ cups all-purpose flour	toasted split almonds

Mix butter, 1 cup sugar, egg, and flavoring thoroughly. Measure flour by dipping method (p. 5) or by sifting. Stir together flour and baking powder; blend into shortening mixture. Chill dough.

Heat oven to 375° (quick mod.). Roll dough 1/16" thick on lightly floured cloth-covered board. Cut with small cooky cutter. Place on ungreased baking sheet. Beat egg white slightly with fork. Brush over cookies. Brush with mixture of ¼ cup sugar and cinnamon. Garnish with toasted split almonds. Bake 8 to 10 min. *Makes about 6 doz. 2" cookies.*

Note: *If you use self-rising flour, omit baking powder.*

FINSKA KAKOR

Make Scotch Shortbread (p. 20)—except roll dough ¼". thick. Cut in strips, 2½x¾". Brush tops lightly with 1 egg white, slightly beaten. Sprinkle with mixture of 1 tbsp. sugar and ⅓ cup finely chopped blanched almonds. Carefully transfer several at a time to ungreased baking sheet. Bake 17 to 20 min., or until a delicate brown. *Makes about 4 doz. 2½x¾" cookies.*

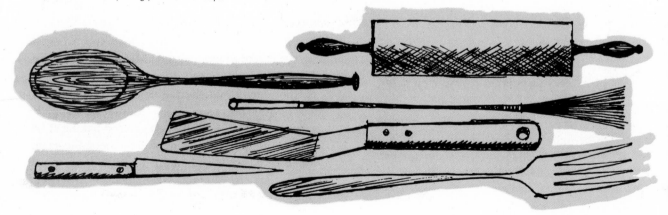

GLAZED OATMEAL BROWNIES

⅓ cup shortening
⅔ cup brown sugar
 (packed)
1 egg
½ cup milk
1 cup all-purpose
 flour
¼ tsp. soda
½ tsp. salt

1¼ cups rolled oats
1 pkg. (6 oz.) semi-
 sweet chocolate
 pieces
½ cup granulated
 sugar
3 tbsp. orange juice
1 tsp. grated orange
 rind

Heat oven to 375° (quick mod.). Grease a square pan, 9x9x1¾". Mix shortening, brown sugar, and egg. Stir in milk. Measure flour by dipping method (p. 5) or by sifting. Blend dry ingredients; stir in. Stir in rolled oats and chocolate pieces. Spread in prepared pan. Bake about 30 min. Just before cookies are done, mix granulated sugar and orange juice. Bring to boil. Remove from heat. Stir in rind. Pour hot syrup over baked cookies. When cool, cut in 3x1" bars. *Makes 27 bars.*

Note: *If you use self-rising flour, omit soda and salt.*

CHOCOLATE CHIP BROWNIE PIE

Make Glazed Oatmeal Brownies (above)—except bake in 9" round layer pan. When cool, cut in small wedges; serve with ice cream.

CINNAMON COFFEE BARS

¼ cup shortening
1 cup brown sugar
 (packed)
1 egg
½ cup hot coffee
1½ cups all-purpose
 flour
1 tsp. baking powder

¼ tsp. soda
¼ tsp. salt
½ tsp. cinnamon
½ cup raisins
¼ cup chopped nuts
Quick Cream Icing
 (½ recipe, p. 151)

Heat oven to 350° (mod.). Mix together shortening, sugar, and egg. Stir in coffee. Measure flour by dipping method (p. 5) or by sifting. Stir dry ingredients together; stir in. Blend in raisins and nuts. Spread in greased and floured oblong pan, 13x9½x2". Bake 18 to 20 min. Cut in 3x1½" bars. Frost while warm with thin coating of Icing. *Makes 2 doz. bars.*

Note: *If you use self-rising flour, omit baking powder, soda, and salt.*

CHOCOLATE PEPPERMINT COOKIES

Refreshing, delightful.

½ cup shortening
½ cup sugar
1 egg
3 tbsp. milk
2 sq. unsweetened
 chocolate (2 oz.),
 melted

1¾ cups all-purpose
 flour
1 tsp. salt
½ tsp. baking powder
Peppermint Filling
 (below)

Mix shortening, sugar, and egg thoroughly. Blend in milk and cooled chocolate. Measure flour by dipping method (p. 5) or by sifting. Blend flour, salt, and baking powder; stir in. Mold in smooth roll about 2" in diameter. Wrap in waxed paper; chill until firm, several hours or overnight.

Heat oven to 400° (mod. hot). With thin, sharp knife, slice dough about ⅛" thick. Bake on lightly greased baking sheet 10 to 12 min. Cool. Place two cookies together with a generous amount of Filling. *Makes 30 cookies.*

Note: *If you use self-rising flour, omit salt and baking powder; bake 8 to 10 min.*

Peppermint Filling: Blend 3 tbsp. cream (12% butberfat) and ¼ tsp. peppermint extract into 2 cups sifted confectioners' sugar. If desired, tint half the filling pastel green and half the filling pastel pink.

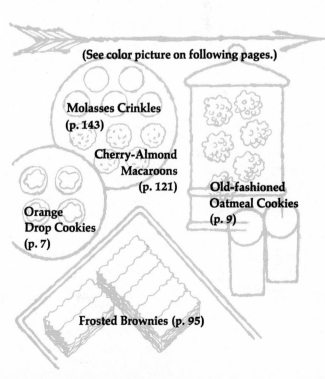

(See color picture on following pages.)

**Molasses Crinkles
(p. 143)**

**Cherry-Almond
Macaroons
(p. 121)**

**Old-fashioned
Oatmeal Cookies
(p. 9)**

**Orange
Drop Cookies
(p. 7)**

Frosted Brownies (p. 95)

BANANA JUMBOS

1 cup shortening (part butter or margarine)	½ cup buttermilk
	1 tsp. vanilla
	3 cups all-purpose flour
1 cup sugar	
2 eggs	1½ tsp. soda
1 cup mashed ripe bananas (2 to 3)	½ tsp. salt
	1 cup chopped nuts

Mix shortening, sugar, and eggs thoroughly. Stir in bananas, buttermilk, and vanilla. Measure flour by dipping method (p. 5) or by sifting. Stir flour, soda, and salt together; stir in. Blend in nuts. Chill 1 hr.

Heat oven to 375° (quick mod.). Drop rounded tablespoonfuls of dough 2″ apart on lightly greased baking sheet. Bake about 10 min., or until delicately browned. If desired, frost with a thin confectioners' sugar icing. *Makes about 3½ doz. cookies.*

Note: *If you use self-rising flour, omit soda and salt.*

INDIAN JUMANAS

South American Indians use achiote, the seed of the annatto tree, to color these tender nutmeg-flavored cookies yellow, and chopped wild spinach for the green color. Food coloring is used for our version.

⅔ cup butter or margarine	2¾ cups all-purpose flour
1 cup sugar	1 tsp. soda
2 eggs	½ tsp. salt
1 tsp. vanilla	½ tsp. nutmeg
½ cup commercial sour cream	yellow and green food coloring
	raisins or nuts

Heat oven to 375° (quick mod.). Mix butter, sugar, eggs, and vanilla until fluffy; stir in sour cream. Measure flour by dipping method (p. 5) or by sifting. Blend dry ingredients; stir into butter mixture. Divide dough in two portions; color half yellow and half green. Drop dough by heaping teaspoonfuls on lightly greased baking sheet. Press raisin or nut meat into center of each cooky. Bake 8 to 10 min., or until lightly browned. *Makes 6 doz. cookies.*

Note: *If you use self-rising flour, omit soda and salt.*

RHUBARB COCONUT COOKIES

Ask your family and friends to guess what gives this cooky its tangy flavor. A new idea for using leftover rhubarb sauce.

½ cup shortening	1 tsp. baking powder
¼ cup sugar	½ tsp. soda
¾ cup corn syrup	½ tsp. salt
1 egg	1 tsp. nutmeg
1 cup thick, cooked rhubarb	¼ tsp. cloves
	1 cup coconut
2 cups all-purpose flour	½ cup raisins
	½ cup chopped nuts

Heat oven to 375° (quick mod.). Mix shortening, sugar, syrup, egg, and rhubarb thoroughly. Measure flour by dipping method (p. 5) or by sifting. Blend flour, baking powder, soda, salt, nutmeg, and cloves. Blend rhubarb and flour mixture together. Stir in coconut, raisins, and chopped nuts. Drop dough by heaping teaspoonfuls on greased baking sheet. Bake 15 to 18 min. *Makes 5½ doz. cookies.*

Note: *If you use self-rising flour, omit baking powder, soda, and salt.*

PEACH COCONUT COOKIES

Make Rhubarb Coconut Cookies (above)—except use 1¼ cups (1-lb. can) drained chopped peaches in place of rhubarb.

EASY CHINESE ALMOND COOKIES

Perfect accompaniment for Chinese dishes or holiday party foods.

1 cup all-purpose flour
½ cup shortening (half butter or margarine)
½ tsp. salt
¼ cup plus 2 tbsp. sugar

½ tsp. almond extract or vanilla
1 egg yolk
1 tbsp. water
¼ cup blanched almonds

Measure flour by dipping method (p. 5) or by sifting. Place flour in bowl. Cut in shortening. Work salt, sugar, and flavoring in with hands. Shape in long roll 1″ in diameter; wrap in waxed paper. Chill about 1 hr.

Heat oven to 400° (mod. hot). Cut dough in ¼″ slices. Place about 1″ apart on lightly greased baking sheet. Brush each cooky with a mixture of egg yolk and water. Press ½ blanched almond in top of each cooky. Bake 8 to 10 min., or until light golden brown. Allow cookies to cool slightly before removing from baking sheet so they won't crumble. *Makes about 2 doz. cookies.*

Note: *If you use self-rising flour, omit salt.*

BROWN SUGAR PECAN ROUNDS

½ cup butter or margarine
1¼ cups brown sugar (packed)
1 egg

1¼ cups all-purpose flour
¼ tsp. soda
⅛ tsp. salt
½ cup coarsely chopped pecans

Heat oven to 350° (mod.). Cream butter and brown sugar thoroughly. Beat egg in well. Measure flour by dipping method (p. 5) or by sifting. Stir dry ingredients together; blend in. Stir in pecans. Drop by ¼ teaspoonfuls about 2″ apart on greased baking sheet. (Cookies flatten and spread.) Bake 7 to 8 min. *Makes about 10 doz. 1½″ cookies.*

Note: *If you use self-rising flour, omit soda and salt.*

CHOCOLATE OATMEAL REFRIGERATOR COOKIES

Pleasing combination . . . oatmeal gives a delightful coconut quality.

½ cup shortening
1 cup brown sugar (packed)
1 egg
1 tsp. vanilla
½ tsp. almond extract

2 sq. unsweetened chocolate (2 oz.), melted
1 cup all-purpose flour
½ tsp. soda
½ tsp. salt
1 cup rolled oats
½ cup chopped nuts

Mix shortening, sugar, egg, and flavorings thoroughly. Blend in chocolate. Measure flour by dipping method (p. 5) or by sifting. Stir dry ingredients together; blend in. Stir in rolled oats and nuts. Mold in roll 1½″ in diameter. Wrap in waxed paper. Chill thoroughly several hours or overnight.

Heat oven to 350° (mod.). Slice dough ¼″ thick using a thin, very sharp knife. Place about 1″ apart on ungreased baking sheet. Bake 10 to 12 min. *Makes about 4 doz. cookies.*

Note: *If you use self-rising flour, omit soda and salt.*

CHOCOLATE OATMEAL BONBONS

Make Chocolate Oatmeal Refrigerator Cookies (above)—except shape dough in 1″ balls. Bake in 350° (mod.) oven 12 min. *Makes 5½ doz. bonbons.*

DELTA BARS

Nutty brown sugar meringue bakes into cooky base to make chewy butterscotch bar. Popular with young and old.

½ cup shortening
1 cup granulated
   sugar
1 whole egg
1 egg, separated
1 tsp. vanilla
1¼ cups all-purpose
   flour

1 tsp. baking powder
½ tsp. salt
1 cup brown sugar
   (packed)
½ cup chopped nuts

Heat oven to 375° (quick mod.). Mix shortening, granulated sugar, egg, egg yolk, and vanilla well. Measure flour by dipping method (p. 5) or by sifting. Stir dry ingredients together; blend into shortening mixture. Mix thoroughly. Spread in greased oblong pan, 13x9½x2″. Beat egg white until foamy. Gradually beat in brown sugar. Continue beating until mixture is stiff and glossy. Fold in nuts. Spread meringue over dough in pan. Bake about 25 min. Cut while warm in 2″ squares. *Makes 2 doz. cookies.*

Note: *If you use self-rising flour, omit baking powder and salt.*

CHOCOLATE LOGS

½ cup shortening (all
   or part butter or
   margarine)
1 cup sugar
1 egg
2 tsp. vanilla
2 cups all-purpose
   flour

2 sq. unsweetened
   chocolate (2 oz.)
   melted
½ tsp. salt
¾ cup nuts, finely
   chopped

Mix shortening, sugar, egg, and vanilla thoroughly. Measure flour by dipping method (p. 5) or by sifting. Stir flour, chocolate, and salt into shortening mixture. Mix in nuts. Shape mixture in rectangle, 12x8″, on well-greased baking sheet. Cover with waxed paper; chill until firm.

Heat oven to 375° (quick mod.). Cut in 48 logs, 4x½″. Place a little apart on ungreased baking sheet. Bake 10 to 12 min. *Makes 4 doz. logs.*

Note: *If you use self-rising flour, omit salt.*

HIS MOTHER'S OATMEAL COOKIES

2 cups all-purpose
   flour
1 tsp. soda
½ tsp. salt
3 cups rolled oats

1 cup shortening
   (part butter or
   margarine)
⅓ cup milk
1½ cups brown sugar
   (packed)
jelly or jam

Measure flour by dipping method (p. 5) or by sifting. Mix flour, soda, salt, and rolled oats. Cut in shortening until mixture is well blended. Stir in milk and sugar. Chill.

Heat oven to 375° (quick mod.). Roll dough ⅛″ thick on lightly floured board. Cut in desired shapes. Place on ungreased baking sheet. Bake 10 to 12 min., or until lightly browned. When cool, and just before serving, put together in pairs with jelly or jam between. *Makes about 4 doz. 2½″ double cookies.*

Note: *If you use self-rising flour, omit soda and salt.*

HURRY-UP CHOCOLATE CHIP DROPS

3 cups graham
    cracker crumbs
1 pkg. (6 oz.) semi-
    sweet chocolate
    pieces

1 can (14 oz.)
    sweetened
    condensed milk
1 can (3½ oz.) flaked
    coconut (1 cup)

Heat oven to 350° (mod.). Mix cracker crumbs, chocolate, and milk in bowl; form in small balls. Roll in coconut. Place 2" apart on lightly greased baking sheet. Bake 15 min. *Makes 3 to 4 doz. cookies.*

SUMMERTIME CHOCOLATE CHIP DROPS

Make Hurry-Up Chocolate Chip Drops (above)—except do not bake. Place coconut-coated balls on baking sheet or in large pan. Refrigerate until firm, 1 to 2 hr.

PEANUT CLUSTERS

See color picture, p. 132.

1 cup sugar
¼ cup butter or
    margarine
⅓ cup evaporated
    milk

¼ cup chunk-style
    peanut butter
½ tsp. vanilla
1 cup rolled oats
½ cup Spanish
    peanuts

Mix sugar, butter, and milk in saucepan. Bring to rolling boil; boil 3 min., stirring frequently. Remove from heat. Stir in peanut butter and vanilla. Fold in oats and peanuts. Drop by scant tablespoonfuls on waxed paper. Let stand until set. *Makes 2½ doz. clusters.*

NOUGAT BARS

3 tbsp. butter or
    margarine
½ lb. marshmallows
    (32)
4 cups corn puffs
    cereal
¼ cup coarsely
    chopped nuts

½ cup shredded
    coconut
½ tsp. salt
4 sq. sweet or semi-
    sweet chocolate
    (4 oz.), melted

Melt butter and marshmallows over hot water, stirring occasionally. Remove from heat. Fold in cereal, nuts, coconut, and salt. Turn out into buttered square pan, 8x8x2" or 9x9x1¾". With hand protected by a piece of waxed paper, pat out mixture evenly in pan. Spread chocolate in a thin layer over top of cereal mixture. Chill until set, 45 to 60 min. Cut in 2x1" bars. *Makes 32 bars.*

PEANUT BUTTER QUICKIES

1 can (14 oz.)
    sweetened
    condensed milk
½ cup creamy or
    chunk-style
    peanut butter

2 cups fine graham
    cracker crumbs
½ cup chopped dates
    or 1 pkg. (6 oz.)
    semi-sweet
    chocolate pieces

Heat oven to 350° (mod.). Blend milk and peanut butter until smooth. Mix in crumbs and dates. Drop by rounded teaspoonfuls 2" apart on ungreased baking sheet. Bake 10 to 12 min., or until light brown. *Makes 4 doz. cookies.*

CHOCOLATE COCONUT DROPS

2 sq. unsweetened
    chocolate (2 oz.),
    cut up
1 can (14 oz.)
    sweetened
    condensed milk

½ lb. flaked coconut
    (about 2½ cups)
½ cup walnuts,
    cut up

Melt chocolate over hot water. Stir in rest of ingredients. Drop by teaspoonfuls on lightly greased baking sheet in shape of bonbons. Place in oven heated to 350° (mod.); turn off heat. Leave in oven until drops have glazed appearance, 15 to 20 min. *Makes about 4 doz. drops.*

Because people on diets often crave forbidden sweets, we offer here a few recipes for cookies for dieters. None is intended as a "prescription cooky," but where ingredients do not conflict with doctors' specifications, these recipes offer a welcome addition to restrictive diets. Such cookies serve the added social purpose of allowing you, your family, or dieting friends to participate when refreshments are served.

SALT-RESTRICTED DIETS

Those on salt-restricted diets will want to try the unique crisp Italian cooky below. You may want to experiment with favorite cooky recipes, choosing those in which a definite flavor such as chocolate or spices would disguise the lack of salt, and using sweet unsalted butter.

BLAND DIETS

Those on bland diets may be served a variety of vanilla or butter cookies, any cooky delicate in flavor and made without nuts—like Banana Bars (below). A few more of that type in this book are: Ethel's Sugar Cookies (p. 18), Spritz (p. 21), Vanilla Refrigerator Cookies (p. 16).

ITALIAN ANISE TOAST

A good conversation piece when served with ice cream, fruit, or cheese.

2 eggs	1 cup all-purpose
⅔ cup sugar	flour
1 tsp. anise seed	

Heat oven to 375° (quick mod.). Grease and flour a loaf pan, 9x5x3". Beat eggs and sugar thoroughly. Add anise seed. Measure flour by dipping method (p. 5) or by sifting. Mix in flour. Bake in prepared pan about 20 min., or until toothpick inserted in center of loaf comes out clean. (Pan will be only ¼ full.) Remove from pan and cut loaf into sixteen ½" thick slices. Place slices on greased baking sheet; bake 5 min., or until bottoms of slices are browned; turn and bake 5 min. more, or until sides are browned. *Makes 16 slices.*

BANANA BARS

Moist . . . like banana cake. For those not on special diets, ½ cup chopped nuts and an icing may be added.

¼ cup shortening	1 tsp. vanilla
1 cup sugar	2 cups all-purpose
2 eggs	flour
1 cup mashed	2 tsp. baking powder
bananas (2 to 3)	½ tsp. salt

Heat oven to 350° (mod.). Grease a jelly roll pan, 15½x10½x1". Mix shortening, sugar, eggs, bananas, and vanilla thoroughly. Measure flour by dipping method (p. 5) or by sifting. Blend dry ingredients; stir into banana mixture. Spread in prepared pan. Bake 20 to 25 min., or until golden brown. *Makes 3½ doz. bars.*

Note: *If you use self-rising flour, omit baking powder and salt.*

DIETS LOW IN SATURATED FATS

Those on diets low in saturated fats have found vegetable oils, such as safflower oil, easy to measure and quick to mix. See the two recipes below. Other cookies which may be low in saturated fats are those made with egg whites, such as Meringue Cookies (without coconut) and Cherry Almond Macaroons (both recipes on p. 121).

CHEWY OATMEAL COOKIES

2 cups quick-cooking rolled oats	¼ tsp. salt
1 cup brown sugar (packed)	½ tsp. almond extract
½ cup vegetable oil	½ cup cut-up dates, if desired
2 egg whites	½ cup chopped walnuts, if desired

Heat oven to 325° (slow mod.). Stir together oats, sugar, and oil in mixing bowl. Beat egg whites until frothy and add to oat mixture. Stir in salt and almond extract. Stir in dates and walnuts. Drop mixture by teaspoonfuls on lightly oiled baking sheet. Bake about 15 min. Cool; remove from baking sheet. *Makes about 3 doz. cookies.*

STIR-N-DROP SUGAR COOKIES

3 egg whites	¾ cup sugar
⅔ cup vegetable oil	2 cups all-purpose flour
2 tsp. vanilla	2 tsp. baking powder
1 tsp. grated lemon rind	½ tsp. salt

Heat oven to 400° (mod. hot). Beat egg whites with fork. Stir in oil, vanilla, and rind. Blend in sugar until mixture thickens. Measure flour by dipping method (p. 5) or by sifting. Stir together flour, baking powder, and salt; blend in. Drop dough by teaspoonfuls about 2″ apart on ungreased baking sheet. Flatten with oiled bottom of glass dipped in sugar. Bake 8 to 10 min., or until a delicate brown. Remove from baking sheet immediately. *Makes about 4 doz. 2½″ cookies.*

Note: *If you use self-rising flour, omit baking powder and salt.*

LOW-FAT DIETS
Those on low-fat diets can enjoy cookies in which beaten egg whites are used rather than whole eggs. Try Sweet Cereal Puffs (below) or Meringue Cookies (p. 121), omitting the nuts (and coconut).

SWEET CEREAL PUFFS

3 egg whites	4 cups fortified whole wheat flakes cereal
⅔ cup sugar	

Heat oven to 325° (slow mod.). In large mixer bowl, beat egg whites until frothy. Gradually beat in sugar; continue beating until very stiff and glossy. Fold in cereal. Drop mixture by teaspoonfuls 2″ apart on lightly oiled baking sheet. Bake 14 to 16 min. *Makes 3 to 4 doz. puffs.*

SWEET DATE PUFFS

Make Sweet Cereal Puffs (above)—except mix ½ cup cut-up dates with the cereal and fold into meringue.

WEIGHT REDUCTION DIETS OR DIABETIC DIETS

Those on weight reduction diets or diabetic diets should be under the care of a physician and should follow his directions. For additional information and diet recipes, you may want to consult the State Board of Health (if your state has one) or the American Diabetes Association, Inc., 18 East 48th Street, New York, New York 10017.

Quick 'N Easy Cookies

How often do you wish for a full cooky jar to meet spur-of-the-moment needs? When the children bring their playmates home and clamor for milk and cookies...when a neighbor drops in to chat...when you'd love to extend an impulse invitation for an evening of playing bridge or watching television? You can be prepared for the hundreds of occasions in every homemaker's life when impromptu snacks are in order if you keep packaged baking mixes handy on the kitchen shelf. Quickly, conveniently, with fine ingredients mixed by silent helpers outside your kitchen, you can make an endless variety of cookies—refrigerated, rolled, dropped, pressed, molded, or in bars. And every one will have the authentic country-kitchen flavor and aroma that reflect your warm-hearted hospitality.

BROWNIE CONFECTIONS

FOR REGULAR SIZE	FOR FAMILY SIZE
1 pkg. (15.5 oz.) fudge brownie mix	1 pkg. (22.5 oz.) fudge brownie mix
¼ cup butter	⅓ cup butter
2 cups sifted confectioners' sugar	2⅓ cups sifted confectioners' sugar
2 tbsp. cream	3 tbsp. cream
1 tsp. vanilla	1 tsp. vanilla
1 sq. unsweetened chocolate (1 oz.)	1½ sq. unsweetened chocolate (1½ oz.)
1 tbsp. butter	1 tbsp. butter

Bake either fudgy or cake-like brownies as directed on pkg. Cool. Brown larger amount of butter in pan over medium heat until a delicate brown. Blend with confectioners' sugar. Stir cream and vanilla in until smooth. Spread on brownies. Melt chocolate and smaller amount of butter. When cooled, spread thin coating over first icing. When toppings are set, cut in 1″ squares. *Regular size makes 64 confections; family size makes 72.*

FUDGE FROSTING FOR BROWNIES

FOR REGULAR BROWNIES	FOR FAMILY SIZE BROWNIES
1 cup brown sugar (packed)	1⅓ cups brown sugar (packed)
3 tbsp. butter	¼ cup butter
¼ cup cream	⅓ cup cream
1 sq. unsweetened chocolate (1 oz.)	1½ sq. unsweetened chocolate (1½ oz.)
½ tsp. vanilla	½ tsp. vanilla

Combine sugar, butter, cream, and chocolate in saucepan. Boil over medium heat 2 min., stirring constantly. Take from heat. Add vanilla. Beat without cooling until thick enough to spread.

BROWNIE DELIGHT

FOR REGULAR SIZE	FOR FAMILY SIZE
1 pkg. (15.5 oz.) fudge brownie mix	1 pkg. (22.5 oz.) fudge brownie mix
1 egg white	2 egg whites
½ cup brown sugar	1 cup brown sugar
½ tsp. vanilla	1 tsp. vanilla
¼ cup finely chopped nuts	½ cup finely chopped nuts

Heat oven to 350° (mod.). Prepare cake-like brownies as directed on pkg.—except omit nuts. Beat egg white(s) until frothy. Gradually beat in sugar, beating until stiff and glossy. Fold in vanilla and nuts. Spread over brownie batter. Bake 40 to 45 min.

EASY BROWNIE VARIATIONS

Simple additions to fudge brownie mix. Follow package directions except . . .

	Regular Brownies (15.5-oz. size)	Family Size Brownies (22.5-oz. size)
Almond	Mark batter in 30 squares; place a whole almond in each.	Mark batter in 40 squares; place a whole almond in each.
Cereal	Gently pat ¾ cup fruit-flavored corn puffs cereal on top of batter in pan. *(See color picture above.)*	Gently pat 1 cup fruit-flavored corn puffs cereal on top of batter in pan. *(See color picture above.)*
Cherry	Add ¼ cup (about 16) chopped maraschino cherries, well drained, to batter.	Add ½ cup chopped maraschino cherries, well drained, to batter.
Coconut	Substitute 1 cup coconut for the nuts.	Substitute 1⅓ cups coconut for the nuts.
Date	Substitute 1 cup chopped dates for the nuts.	Substitute 1⅓ cups chopped dates for the nuts.
Mocha	Stir 1½ tbsp. powdered instant coffee into dry mix before adding egg, water, etc.	Stir 2 tbsp. powdered instant coffee into dry mix before adding egg, water, etc.
Orange	Substitute ¼ cup orange juice for water and add grated rind of 1 orange.	Substitute ⅓ cup orange juice for water and add grated rind of 1 orange.
Peanut Butter	Omit nuts and add 3 tbsp. chunk-style peanut butter.	Omit nuts and add ¼ cup chunk-style peanut butter.
Peppermint	Add ¼ tsp. peppermint flavoring to batter.	Add ½ tsp. peppermint flavoring to batter.

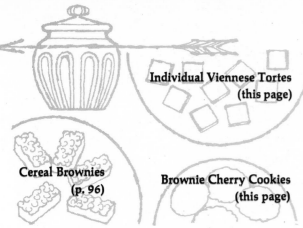

Individual Viennese Tortes
(this page)

Cereal Brownies
(p. 96)

Brownie Cherry Cookies
(this page)

BROWNIE DATE BARS

Heat oven to 350° (mod.). Make fudgy brownies as directed on 1 pkg. (15.5 oz.) fudge brownie mix—except spread evenly in greased oblong pan, 13x9½x2". Mix both date filling and crumbly mix from 1 pkg. (14 oz.) date bar mix, ½ cup hot water, and 1 egg. Spread evenly over brownie batter. Bake 40 to 45 min. Cool; cut in squares or rectangles. *Makes about 30 bars.*

BROWNIE REFRIGERATOR COOKIES

Using regular fudge brownie mix (15.5 oz.), add 1 egg and ½ cup finely chopped walnuts. Or, if using family size fudge brownie mix (22.5 oz.), add 1 egg, ½ cup finely chopped walnuts, and 2 tbsp. water. Mix ingredients thoroughly with hands, adding 1 tsp. water if necessary. Press and mold into 2" wide roll (family size makes 2 rolls). Wrap in foil or waxed paper. Chill several hours or overnight.

Heat oven to 375° (quick mod.). Slice cookies ⅛" thick. Bake 6 to 8 min. on ungreased baking sheet. Cool slightly before removing from pan. *Regular brownies makes 4 doz.; family size makes 6 doz. cookies.*

BROWNIE CHERRY COOKIES

See color picture opposite.

Make Brownie Refrigerator Cookies (above)—except add chopped maraschino cherries (¼ cup for regular and ⅓ cup for family size).

BROWNIE ORANGE COOKIES

Make Brownie Refrigerator Cookies (above)—except add grated rind of 1 orange to batter. If desired, frost with an orange butter icing.

INDIVIDUAL VIENNESE TORTES

See color picture opposite.

Heat oven to 350° (mod.). Using either regular fudge brownie mix (15.5 oz.) or family size fudge brownie mix (22.5 oz.), make batter for fudgy brownies as directed on pkg. Spread batter for regular brownies in a greased jelly roll pan, 15½x10½x1"; for family size brownies, use two greased jelly roll pans. Bake about 15 min. Cool.

Prepare 1 pkg. (15.4 oz.) chocolate fudge flavor frosting mix. Cut brownies in each pan into forty 2" squares. Frost half of brownies (with regular size, half of frosting will be left over). Spread apricot jam, orange marmalade, or peach preserves on remaining squares. Make tortes by placing a frosted square atop each jam-topped one. *Regular size makes 20; family size makes 40 tortes.*

BROWNIE SLOWPOKES

Heat oven to 375° (quick mod.). Follow directions on 1 pkg. (22.5 oz.) fudge brownie mix for fudgy brownies—except omit nuts. For each cooky, place 3 walnuts or pecan halves with ends touching at center on greased baking sheet. Drop rounded teaspoonfuls of dough in center of each group of nuts. Bake 10 to 12 min. If desired, frost with 1 pkg. (15.4 oz.) creamy white frosting mix. Make "turtle" markings on cooky tops with 1 sq. unsweetened chocolate (1 oz.), melted over hot water; apply with tip of sharp knife. *Makes 5½ to 6 doz. turtles.*

BROWNIE DROP COOKIES

Heat oven to 375° (quick mod.). Using either regular fudge brownie mix (15.5 oz.) or family size fudge brownie mix (22.5 oz.), make batter for fudgy brownies as directed on pkg. Batter will be stiff. Drop by rounded teaspoonfuls on greased baking sheet. Bake 10 to 12 min. Cool slightly before removing from pan. *Regular size makes 3 to 4 doz.; family size makes 4 to 5 doz. cookies.*

BROWNIE NUT CLUSTERS

Make Brownie Drop Cookies (above)—except use 2 cups whole nuts instead of ½ cup chopped nuts.

CHOCOLATE FRUIT DROPS

Make Brownie Drop Cookies (above)—except increase nuts to 1 cup and add 1 cup cut-up dates and 1 cup candied cherries.

CRUNCHY BROWNIE TRIANGLES

Heat oven to 350° (mod.). Using either regular fudge brownie mix (15.5 oz.) or family size fudge brownie mix (22.5 oz.), make batter for fudgy brownies—except omit nuts. Spread batter for regular brownies in a greased jelly roll pan, 15½x10½x1"; for family size brownies, use two greased jelly roll pans. Batter will be very thin. Sprinkle with chopped walnuts or finely chopped salted peanuts: ½ cup for regular brownies and 1 cup for family size. Bake about 15 min. While warm, cut in 2" squares; cut diagonally for triangles. *Regular size makes 6 doz.; family size makes 10 doz. bars.*

DOUBLE DECKER BROWNIES

Heat oven to 350° (mod.). Using either regular fudge brownie mix (15.5 oz.) or family size fudge brownie mix (22.5 oz.), make batter for fudgy brownies as directed on pkg. Spread batter for regular brownies in two greased square pans, each 9x9x1¾"; for family size brownies, use two greased oblong pans, 13x9½x 2". Sprinkle with finely chopped nuts (½ cup for regular and 1 cup for family size). Bake 15 to 20 min.

When cool, spread Butter Icing (below) over 1 pan of brownies. Cut in squares or rectangles. Make double deckers by placing an unfrosted brownie on top of each frosted one. *Regular size makes about 3 doz.; family size makes 6 doz. brownies, depending on size.*

Butter Icing (for regular brownies): Blend 1½ cups sifted confectioners' sugar and 3 tbsp. soft butter. Stir in about 1½ tbsp. cream and ½ tsp. vanilla until smooth.

Butter Icing (for family size brownies): Blend 2 cups sifted confectioners' sugar and ¼ cup soft butter. Stir in 2 tbsp. cream and ½ tsp. vanilla until smooth.

UPSIDE-DOWN BROWNIES

⅓ cup all-purpose
   flour
¾ cup rolled oats
⅓ cup brown sugar
   (packed)

½ cup chopped nuts
½ cup butter or
   margarine, melted
1 pkg. (15.5 oz.)
   fudge brownie
   mix

Heat oven to 375° (quick mod.). Mix flour, oats, sugar, and nuts. Pour butter over dry ingredients; blend well. Pack evenly in bottom of lightly greased square pan, 9x9x1¾".

Make fudgy or cake-like brownies as directed on pkg. Spread evenly over oats mixture. Bake 35 to 40 min. Turn upside down immediately. Cool; cut into squares or rectangles. *Makes about 27 bars.*

GLAZED BROWNIES

Follow directions on 1 pkg. (15.5 oz.) fudge brownie mix for fudgy or cake-like brownies. When baked and still warm, spread Glaze (below) over top.

Orange or Lemon Glaze: Mix ½ cup confectioners' sugar, 1 tbsp. orange or lemon juice, 1 tbsp. grated orange or lemon rind, and 1 tsp. soft butter.

ROCKY ROAD BROWNIES

Follow directions on 1 pkg. (15.5 oz.) regular fudge brownie mix for fudgy or cake-like brownies. Frost with Rocky Road Frosting (below).

Rocky Road Frosting

1½ cups sifted
   confectioners'
   sugar
3 tbsp. soft butter
1½ tbsp. cream
1 tsp. vanilla

1 sq. unsweetened
   chocolate (1 oz.),
   melted
1 cup miniature
   marshmallows
½ cup salted peanuts,
   if desired

Blend sugar and butter. Stir in cream and vanilla until smooth. Add chocolate, marshmallows, and nuts.

CHOCOLATE PEPPERMINT BROWNIES

Using either regular fudge brownie mix (15.5 oz.) or family size fudge brownie mix (22.5 oz.), bake fudgy or cake-like brownies as directed on pkg. As soon as they are removed from oven, place chocolate peppermint patties on top, using 16 patties for regular brownies, 24 for family size. Either chocolate-covered peppermint patties or the solid chocolate mint patties may be used. Return brownies to oven for a few minutes to soften patties. As they melt, spread over top with spatula.

BROWNIE CHERRY SURPRISES

Heat oven to 375° (quick mod.). Using regular fudge brownie mix (15.5 oz.), add 1 egg, ½ cup finely chopped nuts, and 1 tbsp. water. Or, if using family size fudge brownie mix (22.5 oz.), add 1 egg, ½ cup finely chopped nuts, and 2 tbsp. water. Blend dough thoroughly with hands. Mold scant tablespoonful dough around drained whole maraschino cherry, completely covering cherry. Bake on ungreased baking sheet 8 to 10 min. If desired, frost while warm with a cherry icing. *Regular size makes 2½ doz.; family size makes 4 doz. cookies.*

BROWNIE MINT SURPRISES

Make Brownie Cherry Surprises (above)—except mold dough around a chocolate mint-flavored wafer, completely covering mint. Do not ice.

DATE BAR DROP COOKIES

See color picture opposite.

Heat oven to 400° (mod. hot). Mix date filling from 1 pkg. (14 oz.) date bar mix and ¼ cup hot water. Add crumbly mix from pkg. and 1 egg; mix thoroughly. Drop rounded teaspoonfuls of dough about 2" apart on lightly greased baking sheet. Bake 8 to 10 min. *Makes about 2½ doz. cookies.*

DATE APPLE COOKIES

Make Date Bar Drop Cookies (above)—except add 1 cup finely chopped unpared apple and ½ cup chopped nuts with the crumbly mix and egg. *Makes 4 doz. cookies.*

DATE 'N RAISIN DROPS

Make Date Bar Drop Cookies (above)—except add 1 cup raisins, 1 cup chopped nuts, 1 tbsp. grated orange rind, and 1 tbsp. grated lemon rind to batter. Bake 10 to 12 min. *Makes 4 doz. cookies.*

PINEAPPLE DATE DROPS

Make Date Bar Drop Cookies (above)—except use 1 can (8¼ oz.) crushed pineapple in place of water; add ½ cup chopped nuts. *Makes 3½ doz. cookies.*

HAWAIIAN PINEAPPLE BARS

Heat oven to 375° (quick mod.). Combine crumbly mix and date filling from 1 pkg. (14 oz.) date bar mix. Mix with ¼ cup hot water and 1 egg. Add 1 can (8¼ oz.) crushed pineapple, drained (about ½ cup), and ½ cup chopped walnuts or pecans. Mix thoroughly. Spread in lightly greased oblong pan, 13x9½x2". Bake 18 to 20 min., or until golden brown. Cool. *Makes about 2½ doz. 3x1" bars.*

LEMON-GLAZED DATE STICKS

Heat oven to 375° (quick mod.). Combine crumbly mix and date filling from 1 pkg. (14 oz.) date bar mix. Mix well with ½ cup hot water and 1 egg. Spread in lightly greased oblong pan, 13x9½x2". Bake about 20 min. Spread with Lemon Glaze (p. 79) while warm. *Makes about 2½ doz. 3x1" bars.*

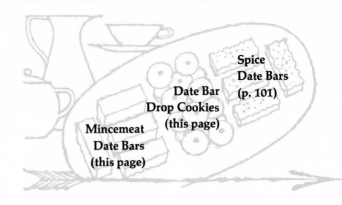

Spice Date Bars (p. 101)

Date Bar Drop Cookies (this page)

Mincemeat Date Bars (this page)

MINCEMEAT DATE BARS

See color picture opposite.

Heat oven to 400° (mod. hot). Combine crumbly mix and date filling from 1 pkg. (14 oz.) date bar mix. Mix with 1 egg, ¼ cup hot water, ½ cup chopped nuts, and 1 cup mincemeat. Spread in greased oblong pan, 13x9½x2". Bake 20 to 25 min. Frost while warm with Thin Icing (below). Cut in bars. *Makes 4 doz. bars.*

Thin Icing: Mix 1½ cups sifted confectioners' sugar, 3 tbsp. cream, ½ tsp. vanilla, and ½ tsp. almond extract thoroughly.

DATE SUGAR BALLS

Follow directions on 1 pkg. (14 oz.) date bar mix—except add grated rind of 2 oranges and ½ cup chopped pecans to date filling. Bake as directed. Cool and crumble. Roll in 1¼" balls; roll in granulated or sifted confectioners' sugar or cocoa. *Makes 2½ doz. balls.*

DATE FILLED COOKIES

Using 1 pkg. (14 oz.) date bar mix, prepare date filling as directed. Stir in ½ cup finely chopped nuts. Set filling aside. Blend crumbly mix from pkg., ½ cup all-purpose flour, ¼ cup soft butter or margarine, and 1 egg well. Chill 1 hr.

Heat oven to 400° (mod. hot). Divide dough in half. Roll very thin on lightly floured cloth-covered board. Cut with 2½" round cutter. Place half the circles on ungreased baking sheet. Spread a teaspoonful of date filling on each; top with another circle; press edges together. Bake 8 to 10 min. *Makes 2 doz. cookies.*

EASY DATE BAR VARIATIONS

Easy additions to 1 pkg. (14 oz.) date bar mix make exciting results. Follow package directions except—

Almond Date Bars	Add ¾ tsp. almond flavoring to date filling.
Apricot Date Bars	Add ½ cup finely cut dried apricots to date filling before adding water.
Candied Fruit Date Bars	Add ½ cup finely cut-up candied fruit to date filling.
Cherry Date Bars	Add ¼ cup chopped maraschino cherries, well drained, to date filling.
Chocolate Chip Date Bars	Add ½ cup semi-sweet chocolate pieces to crumbly mixture.
Coconut-topped Date Bars	Sprinkle finely chopped coconut over bars before baking.
Cranberry Date Bars	Add ½ cup cooked and drained whole cranberries to date filling.
Date Apple Bars	Add ½ cup finely chopped, peeled, tart apples to date filling.
Orange or Lemon Date Bars	Add grated rind of 1 orange or lemon to crumbly mixture.
Pineapple Date Bars	Reduce hot water to ¼ cup and add 1 can (8¼ oz.) crushed pineapple, well drained (about ½ cup), to date filling.
Raisin Date Bars	Add ½ cup raisins to date filling.
Spice Date Bars	Add 1 tsp. cinnamon or ¼ tsp. cloves or ½ tsp. nutmeg to date filling. *(See color picture above.)*
Walnut Date Bars	Add ½ cup chopped walnuts to date filling.

GINGER DROP COOKIES

Gradually add ½ cup lukewarm water to 1 pkg. (14.5 oz.) gingerbread mix. Mix until smooth. Chill. Heat oven to 375° (quick mod.). Drop dough by teaspoonfuls on lightly greased baking sheet. Bake 10 to 12 min. *Makes about 3 doz. cookies.*

EASY GINGER DROP VARIATIONS

Make Ginger Drop Cookies (above) except—

Coconut Ginger Drops	Stir in 1 cup shredded coconut.
Chocolate Chip Ginger Drops	Stir in 1 cup semi-sweet chocolate pieces and ½ cup chopped nuts.
Date-Nut Ginger Drops	Stir in ½ cup dates, finely cut, and ½ cup chopped nuts.
Fruit Ginger Drops	Stir in 1 cup cut-up candied fruit and ½ cup chopped nuts.
Jeweled Ginger Drops	Stir in ⅔ cup gumdrops, cut in small pieces, and ½ cup chopped nuts.
Peanut Ginger Drops	Stir in 1 cup chopped peanuts.
Peanut Butter Ginger Drops	Stir in ½ cup peanut butter (creamy or chunk-style), ½ cup brown sugar (packed), and ½ cup chopped salted peanuts with the water. *Makes about 4 doz. cookies.*
Ginger Creams	Add 1 cup canned pumpkin. Frost tops with Browned Butter Icing (p. 150). *Makes about 4 doz. cookies.*

GINGER-OATMEAL COOKIES

1 pkg. (14.5 oz.) gingerbread mix
1 egg
1 cup applesauce
2 cups quick-cooking rolled oats
½ cup chopped nuts
¾ cup raisins

Heat oven to 400° (mod. hot). Mix all ingredients. Drop dough by teaspoonfuls about 2″ apart on well-greased baking sheet. Bake 8 to 10 min. If desired, ice with Easy Creamy Icing (p. 150). *Makes 4 to 5 doz. cookies.*

GINGERSNAPS

Heat oven to 375° (quick mod.). Blend 1 pkg. (14.5 oz.) gingerbread mix with ⅓ cup shortening or vegetable oil and ½ cup milk. Beat vigorously ½ min. Drop rounded teaspoonfuls of dough 3″ apart on ungreased baking sheet. Sprinkle with sugar. Bake 8 to 10 min. *Makes about 4 doz. cookies.*

GINGER-APPLESAUCE BARS

Heat oven to 350° (mod.). Make batter as directed on 1 pkg. (14.5 oz.) gingerbread mix—except reduce water to ¼ cup; mix 1 cup applesauce, ½ cup raisins, and ½ cup finely chopped nuts into batter. Spread in greased and floured jelly roll pan, 15½x10½x1″. Bake 12 to 15 min. Cool. Frost with Browned Butter Icing (p. 150). *Makes about 4 doz. bars.*

ORANGE NUT GINGER BARS

Heat oven to 350° (mod.). Make batter as directed on 1 pkg. (14.5 oz.) gingerbread mix—except reduce water to ½ cup; fold in 1 tbsp. grated orange rind (1 orange) and 1 cup chopped nuts. Pour into two greased square pans, each 9x9x1¾″. Bake 12 to 15 min. While still warm, frost with Orange Butter Icing (p. 150). *Makes about 4 doz. bars.*

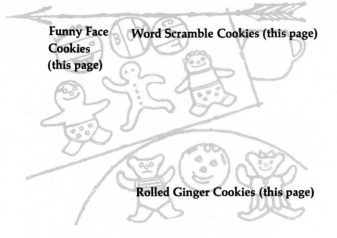

Funny Face Cookies (this page)

Word Scramble Cookies (this page)

Rolled Ginger Cookies (this page)

ROLLED GINGER COOKIES

See color picture opposite.

Add ⅓ cup lukewarm water to 1 pkg. (14.5 oz.) gingerbread mix. Blend until smooth. Chill 1 to 2 hr.

Heat oven to 375° (quick mod.). Roll dough ⅛" thick on floured cloth-covered board. (Use small amount of dough at a time, keeping rest chilled.) Cut out as men, Santas, windmills, or any other shapes as desired. (See p. 103.)

Gingerbread Men: Trace pattern on tissue paper, then cut pattern from cardboard. Grease generously. Place on rolled dough. Cut around pattern with sharp knife. Bake 8 to 10 min. Decorate with icing, raisins, and nuts, if desired. *Makes 18 to 24 men.*

Gingerbread Santas: Cut rolled dough with 4 sizes of round cutters (bottle caps work fine)—2½" cutter for body, 1½" cutter for head, 1" cutter for legs (cut 2), and ¾" cutter for arms (cut 2).

On lightly greased baking sheet, form Santa by pressing circles together. Use scraps for triangular-shaped stocking cap. Use red cinnamon candies to make face and buttons. Bake about 8 min. Cool.

If desired, decorate cookies with cuffs, belt, and trim on cap using Decorator Icing (p. 151). Cut belt buckle from a red gumdrop. *Makes 16 to 18 Santas.*

Ginger Windmills: Cut rolled dough in 3" squares; cut a gash from each corner almost to center. Lift the side of one corner; press point into cooky center. Repeat with alternate corners to give windmill effect. Press 3 red cinnamon candies in center of each cooky. Place on lightly greased baking sheet. Bake 8 to 10 min. *Makes 16 windmills.*

FUNNY FACE COOKIES

Easy-to-make cooky faces that can be used for a fun children's game. See color picture opposite.

Add ⅓ cup lukewarm water to 1 pkg. (14.5 oz.) gingerbread mix. Blend until smooth. Chill 1 to 2 hr.

Heat oven to 375° (quick mod.). Roll dough ⅛" thick on lightly floured cloth-covered board. Cut 3" circles with floured cooky cutter. Place on lightly greased baking sheet. With knife, cut each circle crosswise in thirds and push pieces apart slightly. Bake 8 to 10 min. When cool, frost with Quick Cream Icing (p. 151). Decorate as faces using nuts, candies, coconut, etc. for eyes, hair, mouth, and other features desired. Use your imagination in making surprised faces, happy faces, sad faces, all sorts of faces. (See picture.) *Makes about 3 doz. cookies.*

When you serve the cookies, mix up the pieces from 4 or 5 different Funny Faces. Children can make a game of fitting the pieces together, placing a happy mouth with sad eyes, or a big nose with a little red mouth, in an almost endless variety of amusing faces.

WORD SCRAMBLE COOKIES

See color picture opposite.

Make Funny Face Cookies (above)—except frost cookies with three-letter words, one letter on each piece of the cooky. Beginning spellers will enjoy trading letters to make different words.

THREE-IN-ONE GINGER JUMBLES

Triple the fun . . . sure to please everyone.

Make dough for Ginger Drop Cookies (p. 102). Divide dough in 3 portions and add:

To first portion:
   ½ sq. unsweetened chocolate (½ oz.), melted
   ½ cup whole nuts

To second portion:
   ½ cup flaked coconut
   ½ cup chopped nuts

To third portion:
   ½ cup raisins
   ½ cup chopped nuts

Bake 8 to 10 min. *Makes 4½ doz. cookies.*

BUTTER MIX COOKIES

⅓ cup butter or margarine
½ cup shortening
1 egg
½ tsp. vanilla
1 pkg. (about 18.5 oz.) layer cake mix (except marble)

Heat oven to 375° (quick mod.). Mix butter, shortening, egg, and vanilla. Thoroughly blend in cake mix, ½ at a time. Shape dough in one of the ways suggested below. Bake on ungreased baking sheet 6 to 8 min. for rolled or refrigerated cookies, 8 to 10 min. for pressed or molded cookies. Cool cookies slightly on baking sheet. *Makes 6 to 8 doz. cookies.*

Pressed Cookies: Place dough in cooky press and force through press on baking sheet. *(See color picture, p. 112.)*

Rolled Cookies: Gather ¼ of dough together with fingers. Press firmly into a ball. Roll out ⅛" thick on lightly floured cloth-covered board. Cut with cooky cutters. Repeat using rest of dough.

Refrigerated Cookies: Shape dough into a long smooth roll about 2" in diameter. Roll in finely chopped nuts. Wrap and chill several hours or overnight. Slice ⅛" thick.

Molded Cookies: Add ½ cup chopped nuts to dough. Form scant teaspoonfuls of dough into balls. (These cookies have attractive cracked tops after baking.)

SHORTBREAD

1 pkg. pie crust sticks or mix
1 cup confectioners' sugar
½ tsp. vanilla

Heat oven to 350° (mod.). Prepare pastry for Two-Crust Pie as directed on pkg.—except mix sugar, vanilla, and pie crust mix before adding the water. Roll dough ½" thick on lightly floured cloth-covered board. Cut in rectangles, 1½x1". Place ½" apart on ungreased baking sheet. Bake about 15 min., or until set. Immediately remove from baking sheet. *Makes about 3 doz. cookies.*

ALMOND SHORTBREAD

Make Shortbread (above)—except omit vanilla. Stir in ½ cup chopped blanched almonds and ¼ tsp. almond extract before adding the water.

Freezing Shortbread? Layer cookies between pieces of waxed paper in airtight container or wrap in freezer wrap. Freeze no longer than 3 months. To serve, remove cookies from freezer 20 minutes before serving and place on plate; thaw uncovered at room temperature.

CHOCOLATE DATE MERINGUE BARS

1 pkg. (8 oz.) pitted dates, cut up (about 1⅓ cups)	½ cup butter or margarine
2 tbsp. sugar	1 pkg. (18.5 oz.) devils food cake mix
¾ cup water	1 pkg. (7.2 oz.) fluffy white frosting mix
¼ cup chopped nuts	

Mix dates, sugar, and water in saucepan. Cook over low heat, stirring constantly until thickened, about 7 min. Add nuts. Cool.

Heat oven to 350° (mod.). Cut butter into dry cake mix. Press and flatten all but ⅓ cup cake mixture into bottom of greased and floured jelly roll pan, 15½x10½x1″. Bake 10 to 12 min., or until lightly browned. Spread date filling over baked mixture. Cover with prepared frosting mix. Sprinkle top with remaining ⅓ cup cake mixture. Bake 25 min., or until topping is golden brown. Cool. Cut in 1½″ squares. *Makes 70 bars.*

CHERRY DATE MERINGUE BARS

Make Chocolate Date Meringue Bars (above)—except use white cake mix and cherry fluff frosting mix in place of devils food cake mix and fluffy white frosting mix.

CREAM CHEESE COOKIES

Add ½ cup coconut or chopped nuts to dough for drop cookies, if you wish.

¼ cup butter or margarine	¼ tsp. vanilla
1 pkg. (8 oz.) cream cheese	1 pkg. (18.5 oz.) yellow or devils food cake mix
1 egg	

Cream butter and cheese. Blend in egg and vanilla. Add cake mix, ½ at a time; mix well. If mixer is used, add last part of cake mix by hand. Chill dough ½ hr.

Heat oven to 375° (quick mod.). Drop by scant teaspoonfuls on ungreased baking sheet. Bake 8 to 10 min., until delicately browned. Cool cookies before removing from baking sheet. *Makes 6 to 8 doz. cookies.*

COOKY PRESS CREAM CHEESE COOKIES

Make Cream Cheese Cookies (above)—except use cooky press to shape cookies on ungreased baking sheet. Bake 6 to 9 min., depending on size.

JACK AND JILL COOKIES

Boy and girl faces on rich chocolate-trimmed yellow cookies. Fun to make and fun to serve.

Heat oven to 375° (quick mod.). Remove marble packet from 1 pkg. (19 oz.) marble cake mix. Blend ⅓ cup soft butter or margarine, ½ cup shortening (do not use all butter or all shortening), 1 egg, and ½ tsp. vanilla. Beat until fluffy. Blend in dry cake mix, ½ at a time, beating well after each addition. Knead contents of marble packet and 1 tsp. butter into ⅓ of the dough. Gather half the yellow dough together with fingers. Press firmly in ball. Roll out ⅛″ thick on lightly floured cloth-covered board. Cut 2 or 2½″ circles. Place on ungreased baking sheet. Roll out chocolate dough ⅛″ thick and cut eyes, hair, mouth, etc.; place on yellow circles to make faces. Use your imagination to make each face different. Repeat process with rest of dough. Bake 6 to 8 min. *Makes 5 to 6 doz. cookies.*

EASY CHOCOLATE CHIP COOKIES

½ cup butter or
  margarine
1 cup brown sugar
  (packed)
1 egg
2 cups buttermilk
  baking mix
½ cup chopped nuts
1 pkg. (6 oz.) semi-
  sweet chocolate
  pieces

Heat oven to 375° (quick mod.). Mix butter, sugar, and egg together. Stir in baking mix, nuts, and chocolate pieces. Drop teaspoonfuls of dough about 2" apart on ungreased baking sheet. Bake about 10 min., or until lightly browned. *Makes 4 doz. 1½" cookies.*

COCONUT ORANGE DROPS

Make Easy Chocolate Chip Cookies (above)—except omit chocolate pieces. Blend in 1 cup coconut and 1 tbsp. grated orange rind. Do not overbake—cookies should be soft.

CHOCOLATE-NUT BARS

1 pkg. (18.5 oz.)
  devils food
  cake mix
¼ cup water
2 eggs
¼ cup butter or
  margarine
¼ cup brown sugar
  (packed)
1 cup chopped
  pecans
1 pkg. (15.4 oz.)
  chocolate fudge
  flavor frosting
  mix

Heat oven to 350° (mod.). Mix half the cake mix (dry mix), the water, eggs, butter, and sugar in mixing bowl thoroughly. Blend in remaining cake mix. Stir in nuts. Spread in two greased and floured square pans, 9x9x1¾". Bake 15 to 18 min. Cool. Prepare frosting mix as directed on pkg. Spread over baked layers. Cut in bars, 3x1½". *Makes about 30 bars.*

CHOCOLATE-MOCHA BARS

Make Chocolate-Nut Bars (above). Frost with Creamy Mocha Frosting: Prepare 1 pkg. (15.4 oz.) creamy white frosting mix as directed—except stir in 1½ tsp. powdered instant coffee before mixing.

PEANUT BARS

Prepare 1 pkg. (18.5 oz.) lemon chiffon cake mix as directed; bake in two ungreased square pans, 9x9x 1¾", for 35 to 45 min. Invert to cool. Remove from pans.

Cut in bars, 2¼x1". Frost sides and top with canned vanilla frosting; roll immediately in chopped salted peanuts. *Each square makes 36 bars.*

TOASTED COCONUT BARS

Make Peanut Bars (above)—except roll frosted bars in toasted coconut.

COCONUT SQUARES

Make Peanut Bars (above)—except cut cake in 1½" squares. Roll frosted squares in shredded coconut. *Makes 36 squares.*

BITTERSWEETS

Make Peanut Bars (above)—except cut cake in 1½" squares. Roll frosted squares in 1 sq. unsweetened or semisweet chocolate (1 oz.), grated. *Makes 36 squares.*

CINNAMON BARS

Make Peanut Bars (above)—except roll frosted bars in mixture of 1 tsp. cinnamon and ½ cup sugar.

1-2-3 PEANUT BUTTER COOKIES

1 cup chunk-style
  peanut butter
¼ cup water
¼ cup butter or
  margarine
2 eggs
1 pkg. (18.5 oz.)
  yellow cake mix

Heat oven to 375° (quick mod.). Beat peanut butter, water, butter, eggs, and about half of the cake mix (dry mix) until smooth. Add remaining cake mix; blend thoroughly, using hands if necessary. Drop teaspoonfuls of dough about 3" apart on ungreased baking sheet. Flatten with fork dipped in flour. Bake 8 to 10 min., or until golden brown. Allow to cool a minute or two before removing from baking sheet. *Makes 4 doz. cookies.*

CHOCOLATE CHIP COCONUT CHEWS

Chews made with cherry fluff frosting are pictured on pp. 32-33.

1 pkg. (8 oz.) shredded coconut	1 pkg. (about 7 oz.) fluffy frosting mix (white or cherry-flavored)
1 pkg. (6 oz.) semi-sweet chocolate pieces	

Heat oven to 325° (slow mod.). Place coconut and chocolate pieces in bowl. Prepare frosting mix as pkg. directs. With a fork, stir frosting into coconut and chocolate pieces. With two forks, drop tablespoon-size mounds on lightly greased baking sheet. Bake 17 to 20 min. Allow to cool a minute or two before removing from baking sheet. Store lightly covered with waxed paper. *Makes 3 doz. chews.*

SNOW-CAPPED DATE CONFECTIONS

See color picture, p. 132.

2 pkg. (14 oz. each) date bar mix	1 cup chopped nuts, if desired
½ cup butter or margarine	1 pkg. (about 7 oz.) fluffy frosting mix (white or cherry-flavored)
1 cup water	

Heat oven to 400° (mod. hot). Cut butter into crumbly mix from date bar mix pkg. Reserving ½ cup, press and flatten crumbly mix into bottom of ungreased jelly roll pan, 15½x10½x1″. Bake 10 to 12 min., or until golden brown. Reduce oven temperature to 350° (mod.). Stir water and nuts into date filling (from mix packets). Prepare frosting mix as directed on pkg. Spread date filling over baked layer. Cover with frosting. Sprinkle top with remaining ½ cup crumbly mix. Bake about 25 min. more, or until topping is golden brown. Cool slightly. Cut in 1¼″ squares. *Makes 6½ doz. squares.*

CHOCOLATE CRISPIES

A crunchy cooky—easily made by stirring flour and salt into frosting mix! These cookies store very well.

Prepare 1 pkg. (15.4 oz.) chocolate fudge flavor frosting mix as directed—except use ½ cup soft butter and ⅓ cup hot water; stir in 1 tsp. salt and 2 cups all-purpose flour to make a smooth dough. Shape in one of the ways suggested below.

Heat oven to 350° (mod.). Bake cookies as directed below on ungreased baking sheet. Cool 2 to 3 min. on baking sheet before removing. *Makes 4 to 8 doz. cookies, depending on size and shaping method.*

Rolled: Roll on lightly floured board ⅛ to 1/16″ thick; cut in desired shapes; bake 10 to 12 min.

Molded: Shape teaspoonfuls of dough in balls; flatten crisscross with floured fork; bake 12 to 15 min.

Refrigerated: Form dough in long roll about 2″ in diameter. Wrap in waxed paper; chill until firm, several hours or overnight. Using thin knife, slice about ⅛″ thick. Bake 10 to 12 min.

CHOCOLATE NUT CRISPIES

Make Chocolate Crispies (above)—except add ½ cup finely chopped nuts to dough before shaping.

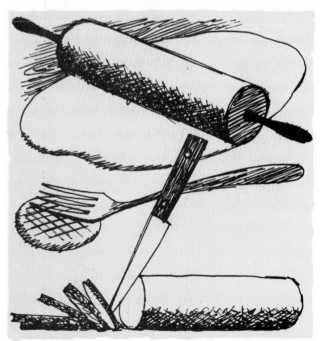

Company Best Cookies

"Company is coming" is a magic phrase which brings an air of excitement to the house, especially to the kitchen. Often it is these company occasions that prompt us to take the time and effort to bake some delicious delicacy. Here, for the four o'clock hostess, are dainty bars, bonbons, and drops—perfect complements to fragrant tea or coffee. Among these teatime treasures you'll find cookies with the distinctive flavors and shapes of foreign lands. Here, too, for hostesses at big affairs, is a variety of cookies to make in quantity. Yes, cookies lend themselves beautifully to easy friendly hospitality. Baked, and even arranged ahead of time, cookies can always be ready to tempt and please your guests.

Afternoon tea is a gracious and elegant way to entertain your friends with ease and at a small expense. Welcome a newcomer to the neighborhood or honor an out-of-town guest at a small tea for twelve. Announce your daughter's engagement or introduce prospective club members at a large tea for fifty or one hundred guests. On these pages are dozens of recipes for fancy, rich, and delicious little cookies to accompany tea and coffee.

CHEESE DAINTIES

A rich, flaky cream cheese cooky with filling of your favorite preserves.

1 cup all-purpose flour	¼ cup plus 2 tbsp. thick preserves, such as cherry
½ cup butter or margarine (¼ lb.)	1 egg white, beaten until frothy
4 oz. cream cheese (½ of 8-oz. pkg.)	granulated sugar

Measure flour by dipping method (p. 5) or by sifting. Cut butter and cheese into flour until particles are size of giant peas. Work dough with hands until it cleans bowl; press firmly into ball. Chill about 1 hr.

Heat oven to 375° (quick mod.). Flatten dough with hand; roll 1/16″ thick on floured board. Cut in 5x2½″ rectangles; spread with 1 level tsp. of preserves, leaving ½″ at edges. Roll up carefully, beginning at narrow side. Seal well by pinching edge of dough into roll. Place pinched edge underneath on ungreased baking sheet; press down lightly. Brush with egg white; sprinkle generously with sugar. Bake about 15 min., or until slightly browned on top. *Makes about 18 dainties.*

Note: *Do not use self-rising flour in this recipe.*

CHEESE TRIANGLES

Make Cheese Dainties (above)—except cut in 2″ squares with knife or pastry wheel. Place ¼ tsp. preserves in center of each square. Fold over, forming triangles; seal edges with fingers or tines of fork. *Makes 3 doz. triangles.*

ALMOND MERINGUE SHORTBREADS

2 cups all-purpose flour	½ cup jam or jelly
2 egg yolks	2 egg whites
½ cup sugar	½ cup sugar
¼ tsp. salt	¼ tsp. cinnamon
¾ cup butter or margarine	½ cup slivered blanched almonds

Heat oven to 400° (mod. hot). Measure flour by dipping method (p. 5) or by sifting. Make a well in center of flour; add egg yolks, ½ cup sugar, salt, and butter. Work together with hands until well blended. Press dough into ungreased square pan, 9x9x1¾″. Bake 15 to 20 min. Cool slightly; spread with jam or jelly. Beat egg whites until foamy. Gradually add ½ cup sugar and cinnamon. Continue beating until egg whites stand in stiff peaks. Spread meringue over jam; sprinkle with almonds. Bake 8 to 10 min., or until meringue is brown. Cut in 1½″ squares. *Makes 3 doz. squares.*

Note: *If you use self-rising flour, omit salt.*

ANGEL SANDWICHES

A cooky to make you famous. From Claire Horsley, Toronto, Canada. See color picture opposite.

½ cup shortening (half butter or margarine)	1 cup cut-up dates
	1 cup raisins
½ cup confectioners' sugar	¼ cup sugar
	1½ cups water
1 cup all-purpose flour	Sweetened Whipped Cream Topping (below)

Heat oven to 350° (mod.). Mix shortening and confectioners' sugar thoroughly. Measure flour by dipping method (p. 5) or by sifting. Stir flour into shortening mixture. Press and flatten with hand to cover bottom of ungreased oblong pan, 13x9½x2". Bake 15 min.

Blend fruit, sugar, and water in saucepan. Cook over low heat, stirring constantly, until thickened, about 10 min. Cool both crust and filling. Spread filling over crust; spread Topping over filling. Chill before cutting in 1" squares. Store covered in refrigerator. *Makes about 8 doz. squares.*

Note: *You may use self-rising flour in this recipe.*

Sweetened Whipped Cream Topping: Beat 1 cup chilled whipping cream (35% butterfat), ¼ cup sifted confectioners' sugar, and ¼ tsp. vanilla (if desired) until stiff in chilled deep bowl with cold rotary or electric beater.

MELTAWAY COOKIES

1 cup butter or margarine	1 tsp. vanilla
	2¼ cups cake flour
½ cup sifted confectioners' sugar	¼ tsp. salt

Heat oven to 400° (mod. hot). Mix butter, confectioners' sugar, and vanilla thoroughly. Measure flour by spooning into cup and leveling off or by sifting. Stir flour and salt together; blend into shortening mixture. Drop by teaspoonfuls on ungreased baking sheet. (Cookies do not spread.) Bake about 8 min., or until set but not brown. While warm, dip in confectioners' sugar. Cool. *Makes 5 doz. cookies.*

GREEN PEPPERMINT MELTAWAY COOKIES

See color picture opposite.

Make Meltaway Cookies (above)—except substitute 1 tsp. peppermint extract for vanilla; add a few drops of green food coloring.

PARTY MELTAWAY COOKIES

Make Meltaway Cookies (above)—except substitute rum extract for vanilla. Top each cooky with half of a candied cherry.

ALMOND MELTAWAY COOKIES

Make Meltaway Cookies (above)—except substitute 1 tsp. almond extract for vanilla. Top each cooky with blanched almond half before baking.

NUT MELTAWAY COOKIES

Make Meltaway Cookies (above)—except add ¾ cup finely chopped nuts to dough.

SPICE MELTAWAY COOKIES

Make Meltaway Cookies (above)—except omit vanilla; add ½ tsp. cinnamon, ¼ tsp. nutmeg, and ⅛ tsp. cloves with the flour.

ORANGE MELTAWAY COOKIES

Make Meltaway Cookies (above)—except omit vanilla; add 2 tsp. grated orange rind and a few drops yellow food coloring.

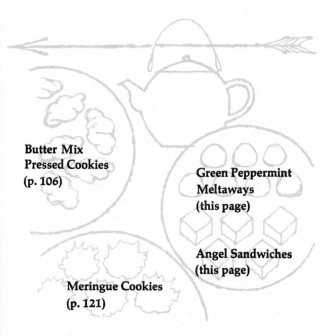

Butter Mix Pressed Cookies (p. 106)

Green Peppermint Meltaways (this page)

Angel Sandwiches (this page)

Meringue Cookies (p. 121)

FUDGE MELTAWAYS

They melt in your mouth. See color picture above.

½ cup butter
1 sq. unsweetened
    chocolate (1 oz.)
¼ cup granulated
    sugar
1 tsp. vanilla
1 egg, beaten
2 cups graham
    cracker crumbs
1 cup coconut

½ cup chopped nuts
¼ cup butter
1 tbsp. milk or cream
2 cups sifted
    confectioners'
    sugar
1 tsp. vanilla
1½ sq. unsweetened
    chocolate
    (1½ oz.)

Melt ½ cup butter and 1 sq. chocolate in saucepan. Blend granulated sugar, 1 tsp. vanilla, egg, crumbs, coconut, and nuts into butter-chocolate mixture. Mix well and press into ungreased baking dish, 11½x7½x 1½″, or square pan, 9x9x1¾″. Refrigerate.

Mix ¼ cup butter, milk, confectioners' sugar, and 1 tsp. vanilla. Spread over crumb mixture. Chill.

Melt 1½ sq. chocolate and spread over chilled filling. Chill. Cut before firm. *Makes 3 to 4 doz. squares.*

Fudge Meltaways (this page)

Chocolate
Refrigerator Cookies
(p. 15)

Chocolate Pinwhee
(p. 11

Chocolate Yummies
(p. 115)

Coconut-Chocolate
Meringue Bites
(p. 116)

WALNUT SLICES

Make Dream Bars (p. 13)—except use 1 cup chopped walnuts in place of coconut and almonds in topping. Frost with Lemon Frosting (below).

Lemon Frosting: Blend 1½ cups sifted confectioners' sugar, 2 tbsp. soft butter or margarine, 1½ tbsp. orange juice, and 1 tsp. lemon juice; stir until smooth.

CHOCOLATE PINWHEELS

See color picture above.

Make dough for Ethel's Sugar Cookies (p. 18), using vanilla for flavoring. Divide dough in half. Blend 2 sq. unsweetened chocolate (2 oz.), melted and cooled, into one half. Chill. Roll remaining dough into an oblong, 12x9″. Roll chocolate dough same size; lay on top of white. Roll layers of dough together until 3/16″ thick. Roll up tightly, beginning at wide side. Chill again.

Heat oven to 400° (mod. hot). Cut ⅛″ thick slices; place on ungreased baking sheet. Bake 8 to 10 min. *Makes 7 doz. cookies.*

HALF 'N HALF SLICES

Follow directions for Chocolate Pinwheels (above)—except do not roll out doughs. Instead shape each half into 2½″ roll; chill several hours. Cut each roll in half lengthwise; press cut surfaces of contrasting halves together. Chill again until firm. Slice and bake as above.

CHOCOLATE YUMMIES

No baking—just melt chocolate and marshmallows; stir, drop, and chill. See color picture above.

1 pkg. (6 oz.) semi-sweet chocolate pieces	½ tsp. vanilla
	1 cup flaked or shredded coconut
⅓ cup butter or margarine	2 cups rolled oats (quick or old-fashioned)
16 large marshmallows	

Melt chocolate pieces, butter, and marshmallows in double boiler; stir until smooth. Remove from heat. (Chocolate-butter-marshmallow mixture may separate but will hold together when rest of ingredients are added.) Stir in vanilla, coconut, and oats. Mix thoroughly. Drop by teaspoonfuls on waxed paper. Refrigerate. *Makes 3 doz. yummies.*

COCONUT-CHOCOLATE MERINGUE BITES

From Diana Williams of San Francisco, formerly of our staff. See color picture, pp. 114-115.

¾ cup butter or margarine	¼ tsp. soda
½ cup brown sugar (packed)	¼ tsp. salt
½ cup granulated sugar	1 pkg. (6 oz.) semi-sweet chocolate pieces
3 eggs, separated	1 cup flaked or grated coconut
1 tsp. vanilla	¾ cup coarsely chopped nuts
2 cups all-purpose flour	1 cup brown sugar (packed)
1 tsp. baking powder	

Heat oven to 350° (mod.). Grease an oblong pan, 13x9½x2". Mix butter, ½ cup brown sugar, granulated sugar, egg yolks, and vanilla. Beat 2 min. medium speed on mixer or 300 vigorous strokes by hand, scraping bowl constantly. Measure flour by dipping method (p. 5) or by sifting. Blend flour, baking powder, soda, and salt together; mix in thoroughly. Spread or pat dough in pan. Sprinkle with chocolate pieces, coconut, and nuts. Beat egg whites until frothy; add 1 cup brown sugar gradually; beat until stiff. Spread over nuts. Bake 35 to 40 min. Cool; cut in bars. *Makes 40 to 60 bars.*

Note: *If you use self-rising flour, omit baking powder, soda, and salt.*

CHOCOLATE ORANGE DROPS

½ cup shortening (part butter or margarine)	1 tsp. vanilla
1 pkg. (3 oz.) cream cheese	1 cup all-purpose flour
½ cup sugar	½ tsp. salt
1 egg	1 pkg. (6 oz.) semi-sweet chocolate pieces
1 tsp. grated orange rind	

Heat oven to 350° (mod.). Mix shortening, cream cheese, sugar, egg, orange rind, and vanilla thoroughly. Measure flour by dipping method (p. 5) or by sifting. Blend flour and salt together; stir into shortening mixture. Stir in chocolate pieces, mixing thoroughly. Drop dough by teaspoonfuls about 1" apart on lightly greased baking sheet. Bake about 15 min. Edges will be delicately browned. *Makes about 3 doz. cookies.*

Note: *If you use self-rising flour, omit salt.*

FANCY FILBERT BARS

Specialty of Jeannette Campbell Ludcke from Minneapolis, wife of a busy executive and mother of three.

½ cup shortening (half butter or margarine)	1 cup all-purpose flour
½ cup sifted confectioners' sugar	½ to ¾ cup currant or raspberry jelly
2 egg yolks	Meringue-Filbert Topping (below)

Heat oven to 350° (mod.). Mix shortening, sugar, and egg yolks thoroughly. Measure flour by dipping method (p. 5) or by sifting. Stir in flour. Press and flatten with hand to cover bottom of ungreased oblong pan, 13x9½x2". Bake 10 min. Spread with softened jelly, then with Topping. Bake 20 min. more, or until Topping is golden brown. Cool slightly; cut in bars. *Makes about 2½ doz. 3x1" bars.*

Note: *You may use self-rising flour in this recipe.*

Meringue-Filbert Topping: Beat 2 egg whites until frothy. Gradually add ½ cup sugar and ¼ tsp. cinnamon; beat until stiff and glossy. Fold in 1 cup finely chopped filberts (unblanched).

CHEESE SWIRL BROWNIES

Golden filling marbled into a delightful cake-like brownie. Developed by Marcia McMullen of Ohio State University while working in our kitchens on a special student project.

Heat oven to 375° (quick mod.). Spread half the Brownie Dough (below) in greased square pan, 9x9x 1¾"; pour Cheese Mixture (below) over. Spread remaining Brownie Dough over top. Pull knife through in both directions to marble. Bake 40 to 45 min., or until toothpick stuck in center comes out clean. Cool; cut in squares. *Makes 3 doz. 1½" squares.*

Brownie Dough

1 cup sugar	1 cup cake flour
½ cup butter or margarine	½ tsp. baking powder
2 eggs	½ tsp. salt
½ tsp. vanilla	1 cup chopped walnuts
2 sq. unsweetened chocolate (2 oz.), melted	

Mix sugar, butter, eggs, and vanilla. Blend in chocolate. Measure flour by spooning into cup and leveling off or by sifting. Blend rest of ingredients thoroughly; mix into chocolate mixture.

Cheese Mixture

¼ cup sugar	1 tbsp. cornstarch
2 tbsp. butter	1 egg
1 cup cream-style cottage cheese	½ tsp. vanilla

Cream sugar and butter. Add cottage cheese and cornstarch; mix thoroughly. Add egg and vanilla; blend well, using electric mixer or rotary beater.

NUT BONBON COOKIES

1 pkg. (8 oz.) cream cheese	2 cups all-purpose flour
1 cup shortening (part butter or margarine)	confectioners' sugar
	9 doz. walnut halves

Mix cheese and shortening with fork. Measure flour by dipping method (p. 5) or by sifting. Mix flour in well with hands. Chill several hours or overnight.

Heat oven to 375° (quick mod.). Roll out ⅛" thick on cloth-covered board sprinkled with confectioners' sugar. (This amount of dough will absorb about 1 cup confectioners' sugar.) Cut dough in oblongs, 3x1". Put a walnut half on each oblong; roll up. Place on baking sheet with end of roll underneath. Bake 15 to 17 min., or until golden brown. Sprinkle cookies immediately with confectioners' sugar. Serve warm if possible. Prunes, raisins, maraschino cherries, finely shredded coconut, pecans, etc. may be substituted for walnuts. *Makes 9 doz. cookies.*

Note: *You may use self-rising flour in this recipe.*

APRICOT COCONUT TARTLETS

½ cup shortening (all or part butter or margarine)	¼ tsp. salt
	1 cup all-purpose flour
1 pkg. (3 oz.) cream cheese	apricot jam
1 tsp. sugar	¼ cup flaked coconut

Mix shortening, cream cheese, sugar, and salt thoroughly. Measure flour by dipping method (p. 5) or by sifting. Blend flour into shortening mixture. Form dough into a ball; chill at least 3 hr. (If desired, dough may be refrigerated about 1 week.)

Heat oven to 400° (mod. hot). Roll dough out ⅛" thick on lightly floured cloth-covered board. Cut with 2" cooky cutter; place on ungreased baking sheet. Top each round with ½ tsp. apricot jam. Bake about 10 min. Remove from oven; quickly sprinkle each tartlet with coconut. Bake 2 min. more, or until tartlets are delicately browned. Remove from baking sheet. Cool. *Makes about 3½ doz. tartlets.*

Note: *Do not use self-rising flour in this recipe.*

FLORENTINES

Developed after Helen Hallbert, our former director, returned from Europe singing the praises of this luscious chocolate-orange cooky. See color picture opposite.

¾ cup whipping cream (35% butterfat)	½ lb. candied orange peel, very finely chopped
¼ cup sugar	2 bars (4 oz. each) sweet cooking chocolate
¼ cup all-purpose flour	
½ cup slivered almonds (blanched or toasted), very finely chopped	

Heat oven to 350° (mod.). Stir cream and sugar together until well blended. Stir in flour, almonds, and orange peel. Drop dough by scant teaspoonfuls on heavily greased and floured baking sheet. Flatten cooky with knife or spatula. Bake 10 to 12 min., or just until cookies brown lightly around edges. Leave cookies on baking sheet for few min. to firm up. Melt chocolate bars over hot water. Turn cookies upside down; spread with chocolate. Allow to dry several hours or overnight at room temperature until chocolate becomes firm. Store in covered container or in refrigerator. *Makes 5 doz. cookies.*

SPANISH ANISE STICKS

2 cups all-purpose flour	¾ cup sugar
1 tsp. baking powder	¼ cup shortening
¼ tsp. salt	2 eggs, well beaten
	2 drops anise oil

Heat oven to 375° (quick mod.). Measure flour by dipping method (p. 5) or by sifting. Blend dry ingredients; cut in shortening until particles are size of large peas. Stir in eggs and anise oil; mix thoroughly with hands. Using ½ dough at a time, roll ¼" thick on lightly floured board. Cut in sticks, 4x1½". Place on ungreased baking sheet, about ½" apart. Brush with soft or melted butter or margarine. Bake 10 to 12 min. *Makes 3 to 4 doz. cookies.*

Note: *If you use self-rising flour, omit baking powder and salt.*

GÂTEAU BONBONS

Tiny frosted filled cookies from France. See color picture opposite.

⅔ cup soft butter or margarine	2 cups all-purpose flour
1 cup sugar	½ tsp. baking powder
1 egg	½ tsp. salt
1 pkg. (3 oz.) cream cheese, softened	⅛ tsp. soda
½ tsp. lemon juice	orange marmalade
1 tsp. finely grated lemon rind	Easy Creamy Icing (p. 150)

Mix first 6 ingredients until light and fluffy. Measure flour by dipping method (p. 5) or by sifting. Blend dry ingredients; add to butter mixture; mix well. Chill.

Heat oven to 350° (mod.). Using ¼ of dough at a time (keep rest refrigerated), roll ⅛" thick on lightly floured board. Cut 1" rounds. Place half the rounds on lightly greased baking sheet. Put ¼ tsp. marmalade in center of each. (For larger bonbons: cut 1½" rounds; fill with ½ tsp. marmalade.) Cover with remaining half of rounds; seal edges with floured finger. Bake 8 to 10 min., or until edges are browned. When cool, frost with tinted Icing. *Makes 7 doz. 1" bonbons.*

Note: *Do not use self-rising flour in this recipe.*

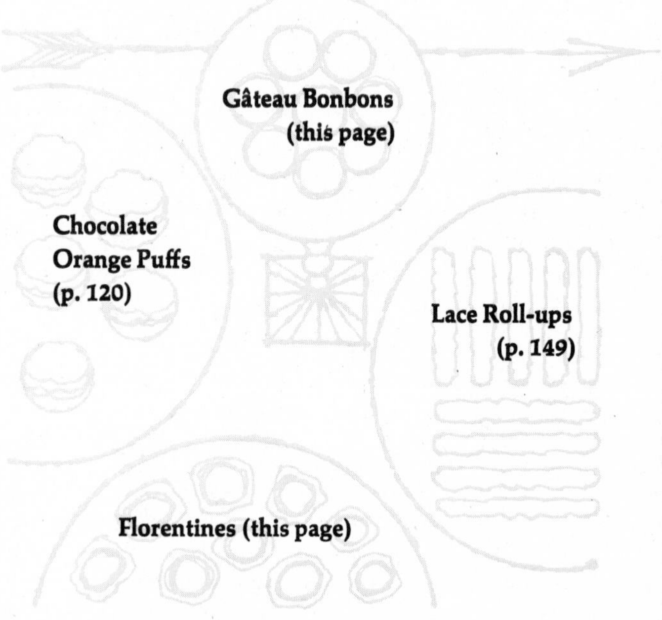

Gâteau Bonbons
(this page)

Chocolate
Orange Puffs
(p. 120)

Lace Roll-ups
(p. 149)

Florentines (this page)

CHOCOLATE ORANGE PUFFS

Orange-flavored miniature cream puffs filled with chocolate cream. See color picture, p. 119.

½ cup water
¼ cup butter or margarine
⅛ tsp. salt
½ cup all-purpose flour

2 eggs
grated rind of 1 orange (2 to 3 tbsp.)
Chocolate Cream Filling (below)

Heat oven to 450° (hot). Blend water, butter, and salt; bring to a boil. Measure flour by dipping method (p. 5) or by sifting. Add flour; stir briskly until mixture leaves the pan and forms a smooth ball, about 1 min. Remove from heat; add one egg at a time; beat well after each addition. Fold in orange rind. Drop dough by level teaspoonfuls on ungreased baking sheet. Bake 12 to 15 min. Remove from baking sheet immediately; cool. Fill with Filling. Refrigerate until served. *Makes 4 to 5 doz. puffs.*

Note: *If you use self-rising flour, omit salt.*

Chocolate Cream Filling: Melt ½ cup semi-sweet chocolate pieces over hot (not boiling) water. Add 2 tbsp. orange juice or water. Remove from heat and cool. Fold in ⅓ cup finely chopped almonds. Beat ½ cup whipping cream until stiff. Fold into chocolate mixture.

ALMOND BUTTER COOKIES

1 cup butter
½ cup sugar
1 cup finely chopped almonds (don't remove skins)

2 tsp. vanilla
2 cups all-purpose flour

Heat oven to 350° (mod.). Cream butter and sugar together. Stir in almonds and vanilla. Measure flour by dipping method (p. 5) or by sifting. Blend in flour with pastry blender. Form in small balls (scant teaspoonfuls). Place on ungreased baking sheet. Flatten with bottom of greased glass dipped in sugar. Bake 9 to 10 min., or until slightly browned. *Makes about 6 doz. cookies.*

PARISIAN ORANGE COOKIES

2 tbsp. coarsely grated orange rind
½ cup water
¼ cup sugar
½ cup butter or margarine

1 cup sugar
1 tbsp. sherry flavoring
1¼ cups all-purpose flour
1 tbsp. baking powder
½ tsp. salt

Heat oven to 375° (quick mod.). Blend orange rind, water, and ¼ cup sugar in saucepan; boil gently over med. heat 10 to 15 min., until mixture is thin syrup consistency. Add enough water to make ¼ cup syrup. Cream butter, 1 cup sugar, and flavoring until fluffy. Measure flour by dipping method (p. 5) or by sifting; blend dry ingredients. Stir syrup, then dry ingredients into creamed mixture; mix thoroughly. Roll in 1″ balls. Place 2″ apart on lightly greased baking sheet. Flatten with bottom of greased glass dipped in sugar. Bake about 8 min. *Makes 4½ doz. cookies.*

Note: *If you use self-rising flour, omit baking powder and salt.*

CHOCOLATE WAFERS

1 sq. unsweetened chocolate (1 oz.)
½ cup shortening (half butter or margarine)
½ cup sugar
1 egg

¼ tsp. vanilla
¼ cup all-purpose flour
¼ tsp. salt
⅓ cup finely chopped nuts

Heat oven to 375° (quick mod.). Melt chocolate and shortening together over hot water. Remove from heat; beat in sugar, egg, and vanilla; blend well. Mix in flour and salt. Spread in well-greased jelly roll pan, 15½x10½x1″. Sprinkle with nuts. Bake 15 min. Do not cool. Cut in 2½x1″ strips; immediately remove from pan. *Makes 6½ doz. strips.*

Note: *If cookies harden in pan before all are removed, place pan in oven a few minutes to soften them.*

CHOCOLATE TRIANGLES

Make Chocolate Wafers (above)—except cut in 2″ squares, cutting each square into a triangle.

KISSES

Moist, chewy, macaroon-like.

½ cup egg whites (4 medium)	½ tsp. vanilla
1¼ cups sugar	2½ cups shredded coconut or 2 cups finely chopped nuts
¼ tsp. salt	

Heat oven to 325° (slow mod.). Beat egg whites until frothy. Gradually beat in sugar. Continue beating with rotary beater or mixer until very stiff and glossy. Stir in salt, vanilla, and coconut. Drop heaping teaspoonfuls of dough 2″ apart on ungreased brown wrapping paper on baking sheet. Bake about 20 min., or until set and delicately browned. Remove paper with baked kisses; lay wet towel on hot baking sheet. Place paper of kisses on towel; let stand 1 min. Steam will loosen kisses. Slip off with spatula. *Makes about 3 doz. cookies.*

CHOCOLATE-COCONUT KISSES

Make Kisses (above)—except stir 2 sq. unsweetened chocolate (2 oz.), melted and slightly cooled, into the batter.

MERINGUE COOKIES

Candied cherries and coconut may be substituted for dates and nuts, if desired. See color picture, p. 112.

3 egg whites	¾ cup chopped walnuts
1 cup sugar	¾ cup chopped dates
¼ tsp. salt	
1 tsp. vanilla	

Heat oven to 300° (slow). Blend egg whites, sugar, salt, and vanilla in top of double boiler. Place over boiling water; beat with rotary beater until mixture stands in stiff peaks, scraping bottom and sides of pan occasionally with rubber scraper. (Meringue will become lumpy if you don't scrape.) Immediately stir in walnuts and dates. Drop heaping teaspoonfuls of dough on 2 lightly greased baking sheets. (Place cookies on baking sheets immediately; bake one sheet at a time.) Bake 12 to 15 min., or until lightly browned. Remove from baking sheets immediately. *Makes about 3½ doz. cookies.*

CHERRY ALMOND MACAROONS

See color picture, pp. 86-87.

1 can (5 oz.) slivered, blanched almonds (about 1¼ cups)	¼ cup chopped maraschino cherries, well drained
¾ cup sugar	
3 egg whites	few drops red food coloring, if desired

Grind dry, crisp almonds through finest blade of food grinder or chop as fine as possible in food blender. Do not chop nuts by hand. Mix nuts, sugar, and egg whites in saucepan. Cook over medium heat, stirring constantly, 8 to 10 min., or until a path stays clean when spoon is drawn through. Remove from heat; stir in cherries and, if desired, coloring. Drop level tablespoonfuls of dough on 2 greased and lightly floured baking sheets. Let stand at room temperature until cool. (This insures rounded macaroons.)

Heat oven to 300° (slow). Bake about 20 min., or until delicately golden on exterior but soft and moist inside. Remove from sheets immediately. *Makes 2 doz. macaroons.*

Note: *When cooked to right consistency, egg white mixture looks like soft mashed potatoes.*

ORANGE ALMOND MACAROONS

Make Cherry Almond Macaroons (above)—except omit cherries and coloring. Grind ¼ cup candied orange peel with almonds. Add 1 tsp. cinnamon, ⅛ tsp. cloves, and ⅛ tsp. nutmeg.

EGYPTIAN ROSE LEAVES

Rose-flavored cookies shaped like rose petals—or leaves, as they are called in Egypt. Since flour is scarce in Egypt, this cooky is reserved for weddings and other special occasions. See color picture opposite.

⅓ cup shortening
1 cup sugar
2 eggs
1 tsp. soluble fluid
　rose (from
　drugstore)

2 cups all-purpose
　flour
¼ tsp. salt
red or pink
　decorators' sugar

Mix shortening, sugar, eggs, and rose fluid until fluffy. (Be sure to use soluble fluid rose for flavoring, as rose water is not strong enough.) Measure flour by dipping method (p. 5) or by sifting. Stir flour and salt together; mix in. Dough will be soft. Chill several hours.

Heat oven to 350° (mod.). Using ⅓ dough at a time (keep remainder refrigerated), roll into balls ¾" in diameter; place on lightly greased baking sheet. Flatten with heel of hand to ⅜" thickness. Cut 2 slits ½" down at top; pinch at bottom to form "base" of petal (see picture). Sprinkle with red or pink decorators' sugar. Bake 8 to 10 min., or until very lightly browned on bottom. (The cooky tops will still be a creamy-white color.) *Makes 2 to 3 doz. leaves.*

Note: *If you use self-rising flour, omit salt.*

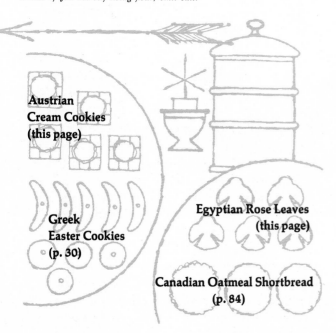

Austrian Cream Cookies (this page)

Greek Easter Cookies (p. 30)

Egyptian Rose Leaves (this page)

Canadian Oatmeal Shortbread (p. 84)

CHEESECAKE SQUARES

1 can (15 oz.)
　sweetened
　condensed milk
½ cup lemon juice
　(2 to 3 lemons)
1 tbsp. grated lemon
　rind
⅔ cup shortening
　(part butter or
　margarine)

1 cup brown sugar
　(packed)
1¾ cups all-purpose
　flour
½ tsp. soda
1 tsp. salt
1½ cups quick-
　cooking rolled
　oats

Heat oven to 375° (quick mod.). Blend milk, juice, and rind until thickened. Mix shortening and sugar. Measure flour by dipping method (p. 5) or by sifting. Stir dry ingredients together; blend into shortening mixture. Blend in rolled oats. Place half of crumb mixture in greased oblong pan, 13x9½x2". Press and flatten with hands to cover bottom of pan. Spread with lemon filling. Cover with rest of crumb mixture, patting lightly. Bake 25 to 30 min., or until lightly browned. Cool. Cut in bars. *Makes 3 doz. 2x1½" bars.*

Note: *If you use self-rising flour, omit soda and salt.*

AUSTRIAN CREAM COOKIES

See color picture opposite.

2 eggs
1 cup sugar
1 cup whipping cream
　(35% butterfat)
3¾ cups all-purpose
　flour

3 tsp. baking powder
1 tsp. salt
Easy Creamy Icing
　(p. 150)

Beat eggs until light. Add sugar gradually; blend in cream. Measure flour by dipping method (p. 5) or by sifting. Mix flour, baking powder, and salt; stir in. Chill at least 1 hr.

Heat oven to 375° (quick mod.). Roll dough out ¼ to ⅜" thick on lightly floured board. Cut in 2" squares. With knife, make two ½" indentations on each side of each square (see picture). Place on lightly greased baking sheet. Bake 10 to 13 min. Cool; frost irregularly with pastel-colored Icing. *Makes about 4 doz. cookies.*

Note: *If you use self-rising flour, omit baking powder and salt.*

KOULOURIA

From Smyrna. See color picture at left.

½ cup butter	1½ cups all-purpose
½ cup sugar	flour
1 whole egg	½ tsp. soda
1 egg, separated	½ tsp. salt
1½ tsp. vanilla	¼ cup sugar

Mix butter, ½ cup sugar, 1 whole egg, 1 egg yolk (reserve the egg white), and vanilla until light and fluffy. Measure flour by dipping method (p. 5) or by sifting. Stir flour, soda, and salt together; blend into butter mixture, kneading to a stiff dough. Chill 2 hr.

Heat oven to 350° (mod.). Shape heaping teaspoonfuls of dough into pencil-like strips (6" long and ¼" thick) by rolling under fingers on floured board. Form in double twist on greased baking sheet (as pictured). Beat reserved egg white with ¼ cup sugar until frothy; brush tops of cookies with this mixture. Bake 15 min. *Makes 4 doz. cookies.*

Note: *Do not use self-rising flour in this recipe.*

BUTTER HORN COOKIES

See color picture at left.

2 cups all-purpose	¼ cup commercial
flour	sour cream
1 tsp. baking powder	½ tsp. vanilla
¼ tsp. salt	½ cup granulated
½ cup butter	sugar
½ pkg. active dry	½ cup finely ground
yeast (1½ tsp.)	walnuts or pecans
2 tbsp. warm water	½ tsp. almond extract
2 eggs, separated	confectioners' sugar

Measure flour by dipping method (p. 5) or by sifting. Stir flour, baking powder, and salt together in mixing bowl. Cut in butter. Dissolve yeast in water; stir in egg yolks, sour cream, and vanilla. Blend into flour mixture. Refrigerate 1 hr.

Heat oven to 400° (mod. hot). Beat egg whites until foamy; gradually add sugar; beat until stiff. Fold in nuts and almond extract. Divide dough in 4 parts. Roll each part into 9" circle on board sprinkled with confectioners' sugar. Cut each circle in 12 wedges. Spread 1 heaping teaspoonful meringue on each. Roll, beginning at wide end. Bake on lightly greased baking sheet 10 to 12 min., or until golden brown. Sprinkle with confectioners' sugar. *Makes 4 doz. cookies.*

Note: *Do not use self-rising flour in this recipe.*

TINY FUDGE TARTS

See color picture at right.

1½ cups all-purpose flour	3 tbsp. water
¼ tsp. salt	1 tsp. vanilla
½ cup butter or margarine	Fudge Filling (below)

Heat oven to 350° (mod.). Measure flour by dipping method (p. 5) or by sifting. Mix flour and salt; cut in butter. Sprinkle with water and vanilla; mix well with fork. Using ½ of dough at a time, roll out 1/16" thick on cloth-covered board generously sprinkled with sugar. Cut in 2½" squares. Spread 1 level tsp. Filling in center of each square. Bring corners to center; seal together. Place sealed side up or down on ungreased baking sheet. Bake 15 to 20 min. *Makes about 2½ doz. tarts.*

Note: *If you use self-rising flour, omit salt.*

Fudge Filling: Mix the following ingredients thoroughly: ¼ cup butter or margarine, 1 egg yolk, ½ cup sugar, 1 tsp. vanilla, ¼ cup cocoa, and ½ cup finely chopped nuts or flaked coconut.

CHOCOLATE-COCONUT CANDIES

From Marie Thorn. See color picture at right.

¾ cup mashed potatoes (homemade or made from instant mashed potato puffs)	1 lb. confectioners' sugar (about 4¾ cups, sifted)
	1 tsp. almond extract
1 lb. flaked coconut (about 4 cups)	Chocolate Coating (below)

Combine ingredients except Coating; drop by heaping teaspoonfuls on waxed paper. Roll in balls; refrigerate ½ to 1 hr. If mixture is too soft to form balls, refrigerate first, then shape balls. Dip balls in Coating, turning to coat on all sides. Keep chocolate over hot water while dipping candy. With tongs or forks, lift balls out of chocolate on waxed paper or cake rack. Place candies in refrigerator to harden. *Makes about 5 doz. candies.*

Chocolate Coating: Mix 2 tbsp. soft butter, 2 tbsp. corn syrup, and 3 tbsp. water in the top of a double boiler. Stir in 1 pkg. (15.4 oz.) chocolate fudge flavor frosting mix until smooth. Heat over rapidly boiling water 5 min., stirring occasionally.

Food plans for large affairs, such as receptions, church luncheons, teas, and club meetings, often call for hundreds of cookies. If you have been asked to be responsible for baking cookies for such an affair, these easy-to-make, easy-to-multiply cookies are just what you're looking for.

ORANGE PECAN COOKIES

INGREDIENTS FOR 5 DOZ.	INGREDIENTS FOR 10 DOZ.
½ cup shortening (part butter or margarine)	1 cup shortening (part butter or margarine)
1 cup brown sugar (packed)	2 cups brown sugar (packed)
1 egg	2 eggs
1 tbsp. grated orange rind	2 tbsp. grated orange rind
½ tsp. vanilla	1 tsp. vanilla
1¾ cups all-purpose flour	3½ cups all-purpose flour
¼ tsp. salt	½ tsp. salt
½ tsp. soda	1 tsp. soda
½ cup chopped pecans	1 cup chopped pecans

Mix shortening, sugar, egg(s), rind, and vanilla. Measure flour by dipping method (p. 5) or by sifting. Blend flour, salt, and soda; stir in. Stir in pecans. Form into rolls 2½" across. Wrap in waxed paper. Chill until firm. Heat oven to 400° (mod. hot). Slice ⅛" thick. Bake 8 to 10 min. on ungreased baking sheet.

FRUITCAKE BARS

INGREDIENTS FOR 3 DOZ.	INGREDIENTS FOR 6 DOZ.
1 cup brown sugar (packed)	2 cups brown sugar (packed)
1¼ cups water	2½ cups water
⅓ cup shortening	⅔ cup shortening
2 cups raisins	4 cups raisins
2 cups all-purpose flour	4 cups all-purpose flour
1 tsp. salt	2 tsp. salt
1 tsp. soda	2 tsp. soda
1 tsp. baking powder	2 tsp. baking powder
½ tsp. nutmeg	1 tsp. nutmeg
½ tsp. cloves	1 tsp. cloves
2 tsp. cinnamon	1 tbsp. plus 1 tsp. cinnamon
½ cup chopped nuts, if desired	1 cup chopped nuts, if desired
confectioners' sugar	confectioners' sugar
Baking pans	
1 oblong, 13x9½x2"	2 oblongs, 13x9½x2"

Heat oven to 350° (mod.). Mix first four ingredients in saucepan and bring to a boil; remove from heat and cool. Measure flour by dipping method (p. 5) or by sifting. Blend dry ingredients; stir into cooled mixture. Mix in nuts. Spread dough evenly in greased pan(s). Bake 35 to 40 min., or until no imprint remains when touched lightly. Cool; sprinkle with confectioners' sugar. Cut in 2x1½" bars. Store tightly covered to mellow.

PETTICOAT TAILS

INGREDIENTS FOR 10 DOZ.	INGREDIENTS FOR 20 DOZ.
2 cups butter or margarine	4 cups butter or margarine
2 cups sifted confectioners' sugar	4 cups sifted confectioners' sugar
2 tsp. flavoring (vanilla, almond, wintergreen, or rose)	4 tsp. flavoring (vanilla, almond, wintergreen, or rose)
4½ cups all-purpose flour	9 cups all-purpose flour
½ tsp. salt	1 tsp. salt

Mix butter, sugar, and flavoring thoroughly. Measure flour by dipping method (p. 5) or by sifting. Mix flour and salt; stir in. Mix with hands. Mold in rolls about 2″ across. Wrap in waxed paper; chill several hours or overnight.

Heat oven to 400° (mod. hot). Cut slices about ⅛″ thick. Place a little apart on ungreased baking sheet. Bake 8 to 10 min., or until lightly browned.

KALEIDOSCOPE COOKIES

We also call these cookies Summer Pastels.

Make dough for Petticoat Tails (above). Divide dough in thirds. Follow directions for 3 variations of your choice (below). Wrap tightly; chill several hours or overnight.

Heat oven to 375° (quick mod.). Hold cookies at room temperature until easy to slice, yet firm. Slice ⅛″ thick. Bake on ungreased baking sheet 7 to 9 min. Do not brown.

Green Cookies

FOR 3⅓ DOZ.	FOR 6⅔ DOZ.
2 tbsp. finely grated lemon rind	¼ cup finely grated lemon rind
green food coloring	green food coloring
multi-colored sugar	multi-colored sugar

Add lemon rind and food coloring to ⅓ of dough. Roll in multi-colored sugar.

Pink Cookies

FOR 3⅓ DOZ.	FOR 6⅔ DOZ.
½ to 1 tsp. pepper-mint extract	1 to 1½ tsp. pepper-mint extract
red food coloring	red food coloring
red decorators' sugar	red decorators' sugar

Add extract and food coloring to ⅓ of dough. Roll in red decorators' sugar.

Yellow Cookies

FOR 3⅓ DOZ.	FOR 6⅔ DOZ.
2 tbsp. finely grated orange rind	¼ cup finely grated orange rind
yellow food coloring	yellow food coloring
finely chopped almonds	finely chopped almonds

Add orange rind and food coloring to ⅓ of dough. Roll in finely chopped almonds.

Chocolate Cookies

FOR 3⅓ DOZ.	FOR 6⅔ DOZ.
2 sq. semi-sweet chocolate (2 oz.), melted	4 sq. semi-sweet chocolate (4. oz.), melted
chocolate shot	chocolate shot

Add melted chocolate to ⅓ of dough. Roll in chocolate shot.

EASY FILLED COOKIES

INGREDIENTS FOR 5 DOZ.	INGREDIENTS FOR 10 DOZ.
1 cup shortening	2 cups shortening
2 cups brown sugar (packed)	4 cups brown sugar (packed)
2 eggs	4 eggs
½ cup water or buttermilk	1 cup water or buttermilk
1 tsp. vanilla	2 tsp. vanilla
3½ cups all-purpose flour	7 cups all-purpose flour
1 tsp. salt	2 tsp. salt
1 tsp. soda	2 tsp. soda
⅛ tsp. cinnamon	¼ tsp. cinnamon
Date Filling (p. 19) or Cherry-Pineapple Filling (below)	Date Filling (double recipe, p. 19) or Cherry-Pineapple Filling (below)

Heat oven to 400° (mod. hot). Mix shortening, sugar, and eggs. Stir in water and vanilla. Measure flour by dipping method (p. 5) or by sifting. Blend remaining ingredients; stir in. Drop dough by teaspoonfuls on greased baking sheet. Place ½ tsp. Filling on dough; cover with ½ tsp. dough. Bake 10 to 12 min.

Cherry-Pineapple Filling

1 can (8½ oz.) crushed pineapple (1 cup including juice)	2 cans (8½ oz. each) crushed pineapple (2 cups including juice)
¼ cup chopped candied or maraschino cherries	½ cup chopped candied or maraschino cherries
½ cup sugar	1 cup sugar
½ cup chopped nuts	1 cup chopped nuts

Mix pineapple, cherries, and sugar; cook until very thick. Add nuts; mix well. Cool.

ORANGE OATMEAL COOKIES

Crispy, crunchy, with pleasing orange tang.

INGREDIENTS FOR 5 DOZ.	INGREDIENTS FOR 10 DOZ.
2 cups all-purpose flour	4 cups all-purpose flour
2 cups sugar	4 cups sugar
4 tsp. baking powder	2 tbsp. plus 2 tsp. baking powder
1 tsp. salt	2 tsp. salt
1 tsp. nutmeg	2 tsp. nutmeg
1 cup shortening	2 cups shortening
2 eggs	4 eggs
4 tsp. grated orange rind	2 tbsp. plus 2 tsp. grated orange rind
2 tbsp. orange juice	¼ cup orange juice
3 cups rolled oats	6 cups rolled oats

Heat oven to 375° (quick mod.). Measure flour by dipping method (p. 5) or by sifting. Blend flour, sugar, baking powder, salt, and nutmeg; add shortening, eggs, orange rind, and juice. Mix well. Stir in oats. Drop level tablespoonfuls of dough on greased baking sheet 2″ apart. Bake 12 to 15 min.

PEANUT JUMBLES

INGREDIENTS FOR 5 DOZ.

⅔ cup shortening
½ cup peanut butter
⅔ cup granulated sugar
⅔ cup brown sugar (packed)
2 eggs
½ cup milk
1 tsp. vanilla
2 cups all-purpose flour
2 tsp. baking powder
1 tsp. salt
1 cup chopped peanuts

INGREDIENTS FOR 10 DOZ.

1⅓ cups shortening
1 cup peanut butter
1⅓ cups granulated sugar
1⅓ cups brown sugar (packed)
4 eggs
1 cup milk
2 tsp. vanilla
4 cups all-purpose flour
4 tsp. baking powder
2 tsp. salt
2 cups chopped peanuts

Heat oven to 375° (quick mod.). Mix shortening, peanut butter, sugars, and eggs thoroughly. Stir in milk and vanilla. Measure flour by dipping method (p. 5) or by sifting. Blend dry ingredients; stir into shortening mixture. Stir in peanuts. Drop teaspoonfuls of dough 2″ apart on greased baking sheet. Bake 10 to 12 min.

MINCEMEAT BARS

INGREDIENTS FOR 6 DOZ.

1½ cups brown sugar (packed)
2 eggs
2 tbsp. molasses
1 tbsp. butter or margarine
1 tsp. vanilla
2 cups all-purpose flour
½ tsp. salt
½ tsp. soda
1 tsp. each cinnamon and cloves
3 tbsp. hot water
¼ cup almonds, slivered
¼ cup raisins
1 pkg. (9 oz.) mincemeat, separated
1½ cups sifted confectioners' sugar
about 3 tbsp. hot milk
½ tsp. each vanilla and almond flavoring

Baking pans
2 oblongs, 13x9½x2″

INGREDIENTS FOR 12 DOZ.

3 cups brown sugar (packed)
4 eggs
¼ cup molasses
2 tbsp. butter or margarine
2 tsp. vanilla
4 cups all-purpose flour
1 tsp. salt
1 tsp. soda
2 tsp. each cinnamon and cloves
6 tbsp. hot water
½ cup almonds, slivered
½ cup raisins
2 pkg. (9 oz. each) mincemeat, separated
3 cups sifted confectioners' sugar
about 6 tbsp. hot milk
1 tsp. each vanilla and almond flavoring

4 oblongs, 13x9½x2″

Heat oven to 400° (mod. hot). Mix brown sugar, eggs, molasses, butter, and vanilla thoroughly. Measure flour by dipping method (p. 5) or by sifting. Blend flour, salt, soda, and spices; stir in. Mix in hot water. Stir in almonds, raisins, and mincemeat. Spread dough thin in greased pans. (Dough puffs and fills in any holes as it bakes.) Bake 12 to 15 min., or until no imprint remains when touched lightly. Spread immediately with mixture of confectioners' sugar, milk, and flavorings. Cut in 2x1½″ bars.

BROWNIES

INGREDIENTS FOR 28 BARS	INGREDIENTS FOR 56 BARS
4 sq. unsweetened chocolate (4 oz.)	8 sq. unsweetened chocolate (8 oz.)
⅔ cup shortening	1⅓ cups shortening
2 cups sugar	4 cups sugar
4 eggs	8 eggs
1½ cups all-purpose flour	3 cups all-purpose flour
1 tsp. baking powder	2 tsp. baking powder
1 tsp. salt	2 tsp. salt
1 cup chopped nuts	2 cups chopped nuts
Baking pans	
1 oblong, 13x9½x2″, or 1 jelly roll pan, 15½x10½x1″	2 oblongs, 13x9½x2″, or 2 jelly roll pans, 15½x10½x1″

Heat oven to 350° (mod.). Grease pan(s). Melt chocolate and shortening over low heat. Beat in sugar and eggs. Measure flour by dipping method (p. 5) or by sifting. Blend flour, baking powder, and salt; stir in. Mix in nuts. Spread in pan. Bake 25 to 30 min., or until toothpick stuck in center comes out clean. Cut in bars; frost, if desired.

CHOCOLATE NUT WAFERS

INGREDIENTS FOR 4 DOZ.	INGREDIENTS FOR 8 DOZ.
½ cup shortening	1 cup shortening
1 cup sugar	2 cups sugar
1 egg	2 eggs
1 tsp. vanilla	2 tsp. vanilla
2 sq. unsweetened chocolate (2 oz.), melted	4 sq. unsweetened chocolate (4 oz.), melted
¾ cup all-purpose flour	1½ cups all-purpose flour
1 tsp. salt	2 tsp. salt
¾ cup nuts, finely chopped	1½ cups nuts, finely chopped

Heat oven to 375° (quick mod.). Mix shortening, sugar, egg(s), and vanilla. Stir in chocolate. Measure flour by dipping method (p. 5) or by sifting. Blend in flour and salt. Add nuts. Drop rounded teaspoonfuls of dough 2″ apart on ungreased baking sheet. Flatten with bottom of greased glass dipped in sugar. Bake 8 min.

MORE LARGE-QUANTITY COOKY RECIPES

DATE-WHEAT FLAKE BALLS

For "children" of all ages.

½ cup butter or
   margarine
¾ cup sugar
1 lb. pitted dates,
   cut up (2½ cups)
1 egg, well beaten
1 tbsp. milk

½ tsp. salt
1 tsp. vanilla
½ cup chopped nuts
4 cups whole wheat
   flakes cereal,
   crushed
finely chopped nuts
   or coconut

Mix butter, sugar, and dates. Cook over low heat, stirring constantly until butter melts. Remove from heat. Mix egg, milk, salt, and vanilla; add to date mixture. Cook over very low heat, stirring constantly, about 4 min., or until dates are soft and blended in with other ingredients. Remove from heat; stir in nuts. Cool 5 min.; stir in cereal. As soon as mixture is cool enough to handle, form into small balls and roll in finely chopped nuts or coconut. *Makes 75 small balls.*

PEANUT-MALLOW CLUSTERS

1 pkg. (6 oz.) semi-
   sweet chocolate
   pieces
1 sq. unsweetened
   chocolate (1 oz.)
1 tbsp. butter or
   margarine
2 eggs

1¼ cups confec-
   tioners' sugar
½ tsp. salt
1 tsp. vanilla
2 cups salted peanuts
2 cups miniature
   marshmallows

Melt chocolate pieces, chocolate square, and butter in top of double boiler over hot water. Beat eggs until foamy; stir in sugar, salt, and vanilla. Blend egg mixture with chocolate mixture. Stir in peanuts and marshmallows. Drop by rounded teaspoonfuls on waxed paper. Refrigerate 1 hr. to set. *Makes 4 doz. clusters.*

ROCKY ROAD CHOCOLATE BARS

For cool cooking, try this bar that is a cross between a brownie and fudge.

1 pkg. (6 oz.) semi-
   sweet chocolate
   pieces (1 cup)
¾ cup evaporated milk
1 cup chopped nuts
2 cups miniature
   marshmallows

4 cups graham
   cracker crumbs
   (52 sq.) or
   crushed corn
   puffs cereal
1 cup confectioners'
   sugar

Add chocolate to milk in small saucepan. Cook, stirring constantly, over low heat until chocolate is melted and sauce is smooth. Mix nuts, marshmallows, crumbs, and sugar in large bowl. Pour chocolate over crumb mixture; mix until all crumbs are moistened. Turn into well-buttered square pan, 9x9x1¾"; press down in even layer. Chill until firm. Sprinkle with confectioners' sugar, if desired. Cut in bars. *Makes 2 doz. bars.*

TING-A-LINGS

See color picture opposite.

Melt 2 pkg. (6 oz. each) semi-sweet chocolate pieces over hot water. Cool at room temperature. Mix 4 cups whole wheat flakes cereal in gently. Drop by table-spoonfuls on waxed paper. Place in refrigerator to set, about 2 hr. *Makes 42 clusters.*

NOODLE CLUSTERS

Make Ting-A-Lings (above)—except use 1 cup Spanish peanuts and 1 to 2 cups chow mein noodles in place of cereal. Drop by heaping teaspoonfuls on waxed paper. *Makes 2 to 3 doz. clusters.*

HAYSTACKS

Make Noodle Clusters (above)—except use 2 pkg. (6 oz. each) butterscotch pieces in place of chocolate pieces.

DATE-COCONUT CONFECTIONS

See color picture opposite.

2 cups walnuts	2½ cups coconut
1 cup pitted dates	2 eggs, slightly
1 cup brown sugar	beaten
(packed)	

Heat oven to 350° (mod.). Grind walnuts and dates in food chopper or chop very fine by hand. Add sugar, 1 cup of coconut, and eggs; mix thoroughly. Drop dough by teaspoonfuls into remaining coconut; shape into balls. Place on lightly greased baking sheet. Bake 15 min. *Makes 4 to 5 doz. confections.*

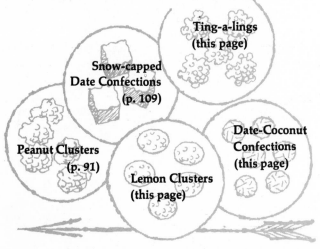

Ting-a-lings (this page)

Snow-capped Date Confections (p. 109)

Peanut Clusters (p. 91)

Lemon Clusters (this page)

Date-Coconut Confections (this page)

ALMOND CLUSTERS

Craving candy? Try this speedy and simple recipe using ingredients from your pantry shelf.

2 tbsp. butter or margarine	1 pkg. (15.4 oz.) creamy white frosting mix
3 tbsp. water	1 cup toasted unblanched almonds
	1 tsp. almond extract

In top of double boiler, melt butter in water. Stir in dry frosting mix until smooth. Heat over rapidly boiling water 5 min., stirring occasionally. Remove from heat; stir in almonds and extract. Drop mixture by teaspoonfuls on aluminum foil or waxed paper. (Keep mixture warm, stirring occasionally, while making candies.) Let cool until set. *Makes 3 to 4 doz. confections.*

CHOCOLATE CLUSTERS

Make Almond Clusters (above)—except omit almonds and extract; use 1 pkg. (15.4 oz.) chocolate fudge frosting mix and 2 cups salted peanuts.

LEMON CLUSTERS

See color picture opposite.

Make Almond Clusters (above)—except omit almonds and extract; use 1 pkg. (14.3 oz.) lemon frosting mix, 1 can (3½ oz.) flaked coconut (1⅓ cups) and ½ cup slivered almonds.

RIBBON FUDGE

In top of double boiler, melt 2 tbsp. butter or margarine in 3 tbsp. water. Stir in 1 pkg. (15.4 oz.) chocolate fudge frosting mix. Heat over rapidly boiling water 5 min., stirring occasionally. Stir in ½ cup chopped nuts. Spread in buttered 8" sq. pan. Repeat with 1 pkg. (15.4 oz.) creamy white frosting mix. Spread over chocolate in pan, making 2 layers. Let cool until set. Cut into 1" squares. *Makes 32 squares.*

CREAM PRALINES

1 lb. light brown sugar (2¼ cups)	2 tbsp. butter or margarine
⅛ tsp. salt	2 cups pecan halves (½ lb.)
¾ cup evaporated milk	

Mix sugar, salt, milk, and butter in 2-qt. saucepan. Cook, stirring constantly, over low heat until sugar is dissolved. Add pecans and cook over medium heat to soft ball stage (234° on candy thermometer), stirring constantly. Remove from heat; let cool 5 min. Stir rapidly until mixture begins to thicken and coats pecans. Working quickly, drop by teaspoonfuls on lightly buttered baking sheet, forming patties. If candy stiffens and is slightly rough looking before all patties are formed, soften and restore gloss by adding a few drops of hot water. Let stand until cool and set. *Makes about 4 doz. pralines.*

BUTTER CRUNCH CONFECTION-COOKIES

Also delicious for dessert; slice ½″ thick and top with whipped cream. See color picture, pp. 50–51.

1 pkg. (8 oz.) dates, chopped	Butter Crunch (below)
½ cup water	1 can (4 oz.) coconut, toasted

Cook dates in water until thick. Cool. Fold in 2¼ cups Butter Crunch and toasted coconut. Roll into cylinder (2″ wide); roll in rest of Butter Crunch to coat outside. Refrigerate several hours or overnight. Slice about ¼″ thick for cookies. *Makes 2 to 3 doz. cookies.*

Butter Crunch

½ cup butter or margarine	1 cup all-purpose flour
¼ cup brown sugar (packed)	½ cup chopped pecans

Heat oven to 400° (mod. hot). Measure flour by dipping method (p. 5) or by sifting. Mix all ingredients with hands. Spread in ungreased oblong pan, 13x9½x 2″. Bake 15 min. Take from oven; stir with spoon. Cool. *Makes 2½ cups.*

PEANUT BUTTER DATE BALLS

1 cup peanut butter	1 cup chopped dates
1 cup confectioners' sugar	1 tbsp. butter or margarine
1 cup chopped nuts (walnuts or peanuts)	¾ bar (4-oz. bar) sweet cooking chocolate

Mix peanut butter, sugar, nuts, dates, and butter well. Break chocolate into top of double boiler and let it melt while shaping dough into marble-sized balls. With metal spatula or knife, spread top of balls with melted chocolate and swirl, giving bonbon effect. Refrigerate until set. *Makes about 110 balls.*

Note: *If chunk-style peanut butter is used, use only ¾ cup chopped nuts.*

PEANUT BUTTER DATE MINIATURES

Follow recipe for Peanut Butter Date Balls (above) —except pat dough into ungreased square pan, 9x9x 1¾″; spread with 1 bar (4 oz.) sweet cooking chocolate, melted. Refrigerate until set; cut into 1″ squares. *Makes about 81 squares.*

CORN PUFFS TOFFEE

Crisp, buttery toffee, mixed with corn puffs cereal. Brittle, but at the same time melt-in-your-mouth.

¼ cup butter or margarine	1 cup sugar
	4 cups corn puffs cereal

Melt butter in heavy 3-quart saucepan over medium-high heat. Stir in sugar (mixture will be very granular). Stir frequently with wooden spoon while mixture melts and begins to turn golden, 4 to 5 minutes (sugar and butter may separate). Continue cooking, stirring constantly, until mixture is light golden and no longer granular, 1 to 2 minutes. (Mixture still may be separated; do not overcook.) Remove from heat; quickly add cereal. Mix until cereal is completely coated. Immediately spread cereal mixture on ungreased baking sheet. Let cool; break into pieces. Store in airtight container. *Makes about 6 cups.*

HOLIDAY APRICOT BALLS

1 pkg. (8 oz.) dried apricots, ground
2½ cups flaked coconut
¾ cup sweetened condensed milk
1 cup finely chopped nuts

Blend apricots, coconut, and milk well. Shape in small balls. Roll in chopped nuts. Let stand about 2 hr. to firm. *Makes about 5 doz. balls.*

Note: *Apricot Balls may be stored uncovered at room temperature for 3 or 4 days.*

TANGY APRICOT BALLS

Make Holiday Apricot Balls (above) adding 2 tbsp. lemon juice to the coconut mixture.

APRICOT-NUT BALLS

Make Holiday Apricot Balls (above)—except add the nuts to the mixture; roll balls in confectioners' sugar.

UNBAKED DATE WALNUT SQUARES

2 cups cut-up pitted dates (¾ lb.)
¾ cup water
2 tbsp. sugar
2 tbsp. lemon juice
¾ cup chopped walnuts
1½ cups graham cracker crumbs (20 2½" sq.)
¼ cup butter or margarine, melted
2 tbsp. sugar
1 tsp. vanilla
½ tsp. cinnamon
¼ tsp. salt
¼ cup chopped walnuts

Blend dates, water, 2 tbsp. sugar, and lemon juice in saucepan. Cook over low heat, stirring constantly, until soft and thick, about 5 min. Remove from heat; stir in ¾ cup walnuts; cool. Blend crumbs, butter, 2 tbsp. sugar, vanilla, cinnamon, and salt. Press ¾ crumb mixture on bottom of greased square pan, 8x8x2". Spoon cooled filling evenly over entire surface. Add ¼ cup walnuts to remaining ¼ crumb mixture; sprinkle evenly over filling. Press entire surface firmly with fingers. Chill about 3 hr., or until firm enough to cut. *Makes about 5 doz. 1" squares.*

Hermits (p. 138)

Cinnamon Jumbles (p. 139)

Oatmeal Drop Cookies (p. 140)

Ginger Creams (p. 141)

Brownies (p. 142)

Chocolate Chip Cookies (p. 144)

Caramel Refrigerator Cookies (p. 145)

Bonbon Cookies (p. 148)

Betty Crocker's Best Cookies

Fashions in cookies—like fashions in women's dress—have changed down through the years. Here is a nostalgic peek at the pace-setting cookies of seven decades. Most of them, having once attained popularity, have continued to fill America's cooky jars as the favorites of each succeeding generation.

Molasses Crinkles
(p. 143)

Salted Peanut Crisps
(p. 147)

Holiday Fruit Drops
(p. 146)

French Lace Cookies
(p. 149)

THE BEST COOKY OF
1880-1890
HERMITS

ONE OF OUR EARLIEST FAVORITES—Rich with spices from the Indies, plump with fruits and nuts, Hermits originated in Cape Cod in Clipper Ship days. They went to sea on many a voyage, packed in canisters and tucked in sea chests.

HERMITS

Spicy, fruity, satisfying.

1 cup shortening	1 tsp. soda
2 cups brown sugar (packed)	1 tsp. salt
2 eggs	1 tsp. nutmeg
½ cup cold coffee	1 tsp. cinnamon
3½ cups all-purpose flour	2½ cups seeded raisins
	1¼ cups broken nuts

Mix shortening, sugar, and eggs thoroughly. Stir in coffee. Measure flour by dipping method (p. 5) or by sifting. Stir dry ingredients together; blend into shortening mixture. Mix in raisins and nuts. Chill dough at least 1 hr.

Heat oven to 400° (mod. hot). Drop rounded teaspoonfuls of dough about 2″ apart on lightly greased baking sheet. Bake 8 to 10 min., or until almost no imprint remains when touched lightly in center. *Makes 7 to 8 doz. 2½″ cookies.*

Note: *If you use self-rising flour, omit soda and salt.*

MINCEMEAT COOKIES

Make Hermits (left)—except omit nuts and add 2 cups well-drained mincemeat to the dough in place of raisins.

NOTES ON NUTMEG

Nutmeg, a popular spice in cooky baking, is one of two spices yielded by the fruit of a certain species of evergreen tree grown in the Molucca Islands. Just under the fruit husk is a red covering that is sun-dried, ground, and sold as the spice, mace. The heart of the fruit is the nutmeg kernel; the larger ones are sold whole, the smaller ones are ground. For freshest flavor, buy whole nutmeg and grate it yourself.

Historical Highlights

1880—*Miss Parloa's New Cook Book,* published and distributed with the compliments of Washburn Crosby Company, forerunner of General Mills.

1883—Brooklyn Bridge, sometimes called the eighth wonder of the world, opened.

1886—The lady with the lamp, Statue of Liberty, dedicated at Bedloe's Island, New York.

THE BEST COOKY OF
1890-1900
CINNAMON JUMBLES

POPULAR COOKY OF THE GAY NINETIES— Every woman and every community had a special version of Jumbles...Bedford Jumbles, Philadelphia Jumbles, Coconut Jumbles, even Wine Jumbles. Though the original was a rolled cooky, our version is a quickly made drop cooky.

CINNAMON JUMBLES

½ cup shortening (part butter or margarine)	2 cups all-purpose flour
1 cup sugar	½ tsp. soda
1 egg	½ tsp. salt
¾ cup buttermilk	¼ cup sugar
1 tsp. vanilla	1 tsp. cinnamon

Mix shortening, 1 cup sugar, and egg thoroughly. Stir in buttermilk and vanilla. Measure flour by dipping method (p. 5) or by sifting. Blend together flour, soda, and salt; stir in. Chill dough.

Heat oven to 400° (mod. hot). Drop rounded teaspoonfuls of dough about 2″ apart on lightly greased baking sheet. Sprinkle with mixture of ¼ cup sugar and cinnamon. Bake 8 to 10 min., or until set but not brown. *Makes about 4 doz. 2″ cookies.*

Note: *If you use self-rising flour, omit soda and salt.*

NOTES ON BUTTERMILK

After Grandmother churned the butter, a delicious and digestible liquid remained in the churn—called buttermilk. It was popular both for drinking and cooking. Though today's buttermilk is cultured from skim milk, it is just as nutritious and just as well liked as an ingredient in tender pancakes and cookies. It's best to store buttermilk in glass, paper, or china because its lactic acid reacts with other materials.

Historical Highlights

1890—Reporter Nelly Bly circled the globe alone in 72 days.

1892—The first practical automobile driven in Springfield, Mass.

1896—A Chinese chef in New York concocted the first chop suey.

THE BEST COOKY OF
1900-1910
OATMEAL DROP COOKIES

FAVORITE COOKY AT THE TURN OF THE CENTURY—The nutlike flavor and chewy eating quality of oatmeal cookies have made them a favorite of families for decades. The tang of molasses and a hint of cinnamon lend delicious flavor to this hearty cooky, selected from dozens of other delicious recipes.

OATMEAL DROP COOKIES

For variety, substitute cut-up dates or finely chopped candied fruits for the raisins.

½ cup shortening	1 tsp. soda
1¼ cups sugar	1 tsp. salt
2 eggs	1 tsp. cinnamon
⅓ cup molasses	2 cups rolled oats
1¾ cups all-purpose flour	½ cup chopped nuts
	1 cup raisins

Heat oven to 400° (mod. hot). Mix shortening, sugar, eggs, and molasses thoroughly. Measure flour by dipping method (p. 5) or by sifting. Stir dry ingredients together; blend in. Stir in oats, nuts, and raisins. Drop dough by rounded teaspoonfuls about 2″ apart on lightly greased baking sheet. Bake 8 to 10 min., or until lightly browned. *Makes 6 doz. cookies.*

Note: *If you use self-rising flour, omit soda and salt.*

NOTES ON RAISINS

When raisins are called for in this book, use seedless raisins; use seeded raisins only when specified. Seedless raisins are grown without seeds while the seeds have been removed from seeded raisins. For variety, you may want to try white raisins, sometimes called muscats, which have been treated to retain their light color. Thanks to modern processing, today's need not be "plumped" and can be added to batters and doughs right from the package.

Historical Highlights

1903—The first successful airplane flight, by the Wright brothers at Kitty Hawk, North Carolina.

1906—Pure Food and Drug Act passed by Congress.

1908—The first Mother's Day observance arranged by Anna Jarvis of Philadelphia.

THE BEST COOKY OF
1910-1920
GINGER CREAMS

COOKY CHOICE OF THE DECADE—Most of the nation's families still lived on farms and in rural areas where molasses was used more commonly than sugar. When chores were finished, children trooped to the cooky jar for cookies like these.

GINGER CREAMS

⅓ cup shortening	½ tsp. salt
½ cup sugar	½ tsp. soda
1 egg	1 tsp. ginger
½ cup molasses	½ tsp. nutmeg
½ cup water	½ tsp. cloves
2 cups all-purpose flour	½ tsp. cinnamon
	Easy Creamy Icing (p. 150)

Mix shortening, sugar, egg, molasses, and water thoroughly. Measure flour by dipping method (p. 5) or by sifting. Stir dry ingredients together and blend in. Chill dough.

Heat oven to 400° (mod. hot). Drop dough by teaspoonfuls about 2″ apart on lightly greased baking sheet. (Cookies will spread slightly during baking.) Bake about 8 min., or until almost no imprint remains when touched lightly. While slightly warm, frost with lemon- or vanilla-flavored icing. *Makes about 4 doz. cookies.*

Note: *If you use self-rising flour, omit soda and salt.*

NOTES ON GINGER

From tropical climates comes ginger, prized for its pungent flavor or "bite." Known since Marco Polo's day, ginger has lent its name to ginger ale and gingerbread. And ginger has found its way into our vocabulary meaning someone who is spirited and lively. Ground ginger, which we use in baking cookies and cakes, is made from dried ginger root. Ginger is also preserved in syrup or crystallized and used as a confection.

Historical Highlights

1910—Fathers honored at first Father's Day in Spokane, Wash.

1914—Electric refrigerator for home use introduced.

1919—World War I ends—American doughboys come home.

1920—Women granted voting rights by passage of the 19th Amendment.

THE BEST COOKY OF
1920-1930
BROWNIES

MUCH REQUESTED IN THE ROARING 20'S—
Legend has it that the first brownies were a fallen chocolate cake. However it happened, brownies are the first choice for picnic baskets, carried lunches, and boxes from home. They still head the cooky "hit parade" today.

BROWNIES

Men love them—so do women and children! The ideal just-a-bite-to-eat for everyone.

4 sq. unsweetened chocolate (4 oz.)	1¼ cups all-purpose flour
⅔ cup shortening	1 tsp. baking powder
2 cups sugar	1 tsp. salt
4 eggs	1 cup chopped nuts
1 tsp. vanilla	

Heat oven to 350° (mod.). Grease oblong pan, 13x9½x2". Melt chocolate and shortening over low heat. Beat in sugar, eggs, and vanilla. Measure flour by dipping method (p. 5) or by sifting. Stir flour, baking powder, and salt together; blend in. Mix in nuts. Spread in pan. Bake 30 min., or until brownies pull away from sides of pan. Do not overbake. Cool slightly and cut in bars. *Makes 32 brownies.*

Note: *If you use self-rising flour, omit baking powder and salt.*

COCOA BROWNIES

½ cup shortening	½ cup cocoa
1 cup sugar	½ tsp. baking powder
2 eggs	½ tsp. salt
1 tsp. vanilla	½ cup chopped walnuts
⅔ cup all-purpose flour	

Heat oven to 350° (mod.). Mix shortening, sugar, eggs, and vanilla until well blended. Measure flour by dipping method (p. 5) or by sifting. Blend dry ingredients; mix in. Stir in nuts. Spread in well-greased pan, 8x8x2". Bake about 30 min. Cool; cut in 2" squares. *Makes 16 brownies.*

Note: *If you use self-rising flour, omit baking powder and salt.*

Historical Highlights

1920—First Assembly League of Nations met in Geneva.

1921—Ladies swooned at first showing of "The Sheik" with Rudolf Valentino.

1922—Emily Post's famous etiquette book published.

1924—Cooking School of the Air launched; this unique service continued until 1948 with over one million women taking part.

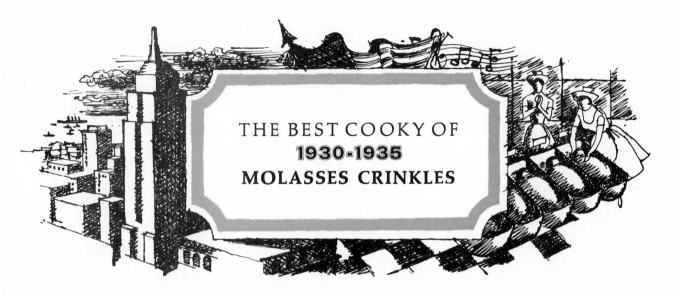

THE BEST COOKY OF
1930-1935
MOLASSES CRINKLES

COOKIES BANISH DEPRESSION BLUES—After the stock market crash, money was scarce and families enjoyed simple pleasures like reading aloud, taking nature hikes, and visiting friends—all occasions for chewy, hearty cookies like these.

MOLASSES CRINKLES

Thick, chewy cookies with crackled sugary tops. Perfect for an after-school snack with cold milk. See color picture, pp. 86-87.

¾ cup soft shortening	2 tsp. soda
1 cup brown sugar (packed)	¼ tsp. salt
	½ tsp. cloves
1 egg	1 tsp. cinnamon
¼ cup molasses	1 tsp. ginger
2¼ cups all-purpose flour	granulated sugar

Mix shortening, sugar, egg, and molasses thoroughly. Measure flour by dipping method (p. 5) or by sifting. Blend all dry ingredients; stir in. Chill.

Heat oven to 375° (quick mod.). Roll dough in 1¼" balls. Dip tops in sugar. Place balls, sugared side up, 3" apart on greased baking sheet. Sprinkle each with 2 or 3 drops of water. Bake 10 to 12 min., or just until set but not hard. *Makes 4 doz. cookies.*

Note: *If you use self-rising flour, omit salt and reduce soda to 1 tsp.*

NOTES ON MOLASSES

Molasses was the chief sweetener in American homes in the 18th and early 19th centuries. Every cabin and covered wagon had its molasses jug; it was used in baking and eaten on flapjacks and on bread. Today, molasses is used more for its rich, mellow flavor than for its sweetening. In recipes in this book, use light molasses unless dark molasses is specified. Light molasses comes from the first boil of the sugar cane stalks; dark from the second.

Historical Highlights

1931—"Star-Spangled Banner," written in 1814, made the national anthem.

1932—The Empire State Building was completed.

1933—Franklin Delano Roosevelt became President, started the New Deal.

1934—Dionne quintuplets born.

THE BEST COOKY OF 1935-1940 CHOCOLATE CHIP COOKIES

NEW COOKY SWEEPS THE NATION—This luscious cooky from the New England Toll House, Whitman, Mass., enjoyed immediate and continuing popularity. It was introduced to homemakers in 1939 on our radio series "Famous Foods from Famous Places."

CHOCOLATE CHIP COOKIES

⅔ cup shortening (part butter or margarine)
½ cup granulated sugar
½ cup brown sugar (packed)
1 egg
1 tsp. vanilla

1½ cups all-purpose flour
½ tsp. soda
½ tsp. salt
½ cup chopped nuts
1 pkg. (6 oz.) semi-sweet chocolate pieces (1 cup)

Heat oven to 375° (quick mod.). Mix shortening, sugars, egg, and vanilla thoroughly. Measure flour by dipping method (p. 5) or by sifting. (For a softer, rounded cooky, add ¼ cup more flour.) Stir dry ingredients together; blend in. Mix in nuts and chocolate pieces. Drop rounded teaspoonfuls of dough about 2" apart on ungreased baking sheet. Bake 8 to 10 min., or until delicately browned. (Cookies should still be soft.) Cool slightly before removing from baking sheet. *Makes 4 to 5 doz. 2" cookies.*

Note: *If you use self-rising flour, omit soda and salt.*

CHOCOLATE CHIP BARS

Make dough for Chocolate Chip Cookies (left)—except spread in greased oblong pan, 13x9½x2". Bake in 375° oven 20 to 25 min. *Makes 48 bars.*

SURPRISE COOKIES

Make Chocolate Chip Cookies (left)—except use 1¼ cups chocolate-covered raisins or chocolate-covered peanuts in place of chocolate pieces.

CHOCOLATE CHIP PEPPERMINT COOKIES

Make Chocolate Chip Cookies (left)—except add ½ cup crushed peppermint-stick candy.

Historical Highlights

1935—Will Rogers, beloved humorist, killed in an air crash.

1936—Edward VIII abdicates the British throne to marry the woman he loves; later they became the Duke and Duchess of Windsor.

1938—Premiere of "Gone with the Wind," later to become the most popular motion picture of all time.

THE BEST COOKY OF
1940-1945
CARAMEL REFRIGERATOR COOKIES

WAR EFFORT BRINGS SIMPLIFIED BAKING—
Men went off to war and women took their places in
the production lines. Thus, cooky baking and other
home tasks had to be speeded up. Refrigerator cookies like these were popular because the dough could
be mixed one day, sliced and baked the next.

CARAMEL REFRIGERATOR COOKIES

½ cup shortening (part butter or margarine)	½ tsp. vanilla
	1¾ cups all-purpose flour
1 cup brown sugar (packed)	½ tsp. soda
	¼ tsp. salt
1 egg	

Mix shortening, sugar, egg, and vanilla thoroughly.
Measure flour by dipping method (p. 5) or by sifting.
Stir flour, soda, and salt together; stir in. Form in roll
2½" across. Wrap in waxed paper. Chill until firm.
   Heat oven to 400° (mod. hot). Cut in ⅛" slices.
Place slices a little apart on ungreased baking sheet.
Bake 8 to 10 min., or until lightly browned. *Makes
about 5 doz. cookies.*

Note: *If you use self-rising flour, omit soda and salt.*

CARAMEL-NUT COOKIES

Make Caramel Refrigerator Cookies (above)—except
add 1 cup finely chopped nuts. Form in 2" rolls.
Makes 6½ doz. cookies.

CARAMEL COOKY TARTS

Make Caramel Refrigerator Cookies (left)—except
spoon 1 tsp. jam on half of slices, top with rest of
slices; seal edges. Cut slits in top so filling shows
through. Bake. *Makes 2½ doz. cookies.*

RIBBON BAR COOKIES

Make Caramel Refrigerator Cookies (left)—except
divide dough in half. To one half add ½ sq. unsweetened chocolate (½ oz.), melted. Form each half
in 2 strips, 2" wide and ¼" thick. Pile strips, alternating colors. Press together. *Makes 5 doz. cookies.*

Historical Highlights

1941—America enters World War II after
attack on Pearl Harbor.

1942—Wartime food rationing required
women to make the best use of scarce
foods.

1945—World War II ends—May 8, VE Day;
September 2, VJ Day.

1945—46 nations convened in San Francisco
to write the Charter of the United
Nations.

THE BEST COOKY OF
1945-1950
HOLIDAY FRUIT DROPS

NATION ENJOYS POST-WAR BOOM—With the boys back home and sugar no longer rationed, Christmas holidays were happy indeed. Rich, colorful cookies like these were perfect for all types of holiday hospitality.

HOLIDAY FRUIT DROPS

One of our best-loved Christmas-time cookies—and one of the easiest to make. They keep beautifully, actually improving with storing. See color picture, pp. 50-51.

1 cup shortening	1 tsp. soda
2 cups brown sugar (packed)	1 tsp. salt
2 eggs	1½ cups broken pecans
½ cup buttermilk or water	2 cups candied cherries, halved
3½ cups all-purpose flour	2 cups cut-up dates

Mix shortening, sugar, and eggs well. Stir in buttermilk. Measure flour by dipping method (p. 5) or by sifting. Blend dry ingredients; stir in. Stir in pecans, cherries, and dates. Chill at least 1 hr.

Heat oven to 400° (mod. hot). Drop rounded teaspoonfuls of dough about 2" apart on lightly greased baking sheet. Place a pecan half on each cooky, if desired. Bake 8 to 10 min., until almost no imprint remains when touched lightly. *Makes about 8 doz. cookies.*

Note: *If you use self-rising flour, omit soda and salt.*

DATA ON DATES

Dates, the fruit of the date palm, have been eaten and enjoyed for thousands of years. To cut up dates for use in a dessert or salad or in cookies: spread pitted dates on a board and cut with a sharp knife, or cut one by one with kitchen shears. When knife or shears gets sticky, rinse in cold water. Since they are expensive, store dates carefully in the refrigerator or in a cool, dry place.

Historical Highlights

1946—Home freezers introduced, promising greater mealtime variety.

1947—Dior's "New Look" exploded upon the fashion world; skirts plummeted overnight, almost skimming the ankles.

1948—Chiffon cake introduced, the first new cake in 100 years.

1950—First transatlantic jet flight completed.

THE BEST COOKY OF
1950-1955
SALTED PEANUT CRISPS

COOKIES PLEASE THE YOUNGER SET—The baby boom, begun following World War II, continues in the new decade. With "kids" in the house, cookies disappear like magic and "moms" need quick and easy cookies like this one.

SALTED PEANUT CRISPS

One of our home testers wrote, "My 13-year-old son carried them out by the handful." "Only modesty prevents me from calling them perfect plus," said another tester.

1 cup shortening (part butter or margarine)	2 tsp. vanilla
	3 cups all-purpose flour
1½ cups brown sugar (packed)	½ tsp. soda
	1 tsp. salt
2 eggs	2 cups salted peanuts

Heat oven to 375° (quick mod.). Mix shortening, sugar, eggs, and vanilla thoroughly. Measure flour by dipping method (p. 5) or by sifting. Blend together flour, soda, and salt; stir in. Mix in peanuts. Drop rounded teaspoonfuls of dough about 2″ apart on lightly greased baking sheet. Flatten with bottom of greased glass dipped in sugar. Bake 8 to 10 min., or until golden brown. *Makes about 6 doz. 2″ cookies.*

Note: *If you use self-rising flour, omit soda and salt.*

NOTES ON PEANUTS

Did you know that peanuts are not really nuts? They are legumes. Like the other legumes, peas or beans, they are rich in protein; like nuts, they are rich in oil. The flavor of peanuts, in fact of all nuts, depends on their oil. If the oil becomes rancid, the nuts are stale and have an "off" flavor if used in baking. To keep shelled nuts fresh, store in airtight jars in a cool, dry place or in the refrigerator.

Historical Highlights

1951—Transcontinental television inaugurated.

1953—Elizabeth II crowned at Westminster Abbey.

1953—Armistice signed, ending conflict over Korea.

1953—Mt. Everest, highest point on earth, conquered by man.

THE BEST COOKY OF
1955-1960
BONBON COOKIES

CANDY-LIKE COOKIES IN VOGUE—Women were fascinated by these beautiful and delicious cookies which were baked as cookies, served and eaten as candies. Excitement over Bonbons brought more candy-cookies, Toffee Squares and Cream Filberts, for example.

BONBON COOKIES

½ cup butter or margarine	fillings: candied or maraschino cherries, pitted dates, nuts, or chocolate pieces
¾ cup sifted confectioners' sugar	
1 tbsp. vanilla (3 tsp.)	
food coloring, if desired	Bonbon Icing (right)
1½ cups all-purpose flour	toppings: chopped nuts, coconut, colored sugar
⅛ tsp. salt	

Mix butter, sugar, vanilla, and food coloring. Measure flour by dipping method (p. 5) or by sifting. Blend flour and salt in thoroughly with hand. If dough is dry, add 1 to 2 tbsp. cream.

Heat oven to 350° (mod.). For each cooky, wrap 1 level tablespoonful dough around a filling suggested above. Bake 1″ apart on ungreased baking sheet 12 to 15 min., or until set but not brown. Cool; dip tops of cookies in Icing. Decorate each cooky with one of the toppings suggested above. *Makes 20 to 25 cookies.*

Note: *Do not use self-rising flour in this recipe.*

Bonbon Icing: Mix 1 cup sifted confectioners' sugar, 2½ tbsp. cream, 1 tsp. vanilla, and red, green, or yellow food coloring, if desired.

Chocolate Bonbon Icing: Make Bonbon Icing (above) —except add 1 sq. unsweetened chocolate (1 oz.), melted, and use 3 tbsp. cream.

CHOCOLATE BONBONS

Make Bonbon Cookies (left)—except blend in 1 sq. unsweetened chocolate (1 oz.), melted.

PENUCHE BONBONS

Make Bonbon Cookies (left)—except use ½ cup brown sugar (packed) in place of confectioners' sugar.

Historical Highlights

1957—Sputnik I, man-made satellite, launched by Soviet scientists.

1959—Alaska and Hawaii proclaimed 49th and 50th states.

1959—St. Lawrence Seaway opened.

THE BEST COOKY OF 1960-1970 FRENCH LACE COOKIES

JET TRAVEL BRINGS NATIONS CLOSER—Fast, easy transportation and more leisure time make travel abroad increasingly attractive. Sampling the cuisine as well as the culture, jet travelers return home wanting to imitate or adapt the exciting and unusual food they've enjoyed in other countries. (See the index for cookies from other lands.)

FRENCH LACE COOKIES

An easy recipe for a famous cooky. The thin batter is transformed, in baking, into a crisp round with open spaces resembling lace. The rolled-up version is popular in Sweden; cooks there roll the warm cookies around a piece of broom handle.

1 cup all-purpose flour	½ cup corn syrup
1 cup finely chopped nuts	½ cup shortening
	⅔ cup brown sugar (packed)

Heat oven to 375° (quick mod.). Measure flour by dipping method (p. 5) or by sifting. Blend flour and nuts. Bring corn syrup, shortening, and sugar to boil in saucepan over medium heat, stirring constantly. Remove from heat; gradually stir in flour and nuts. Drop batter by level teaspoonfuls about 3″ apart on lightly greased baking sheet. (Bake only 8 to 9 cookies at a time.) Bake 5 to 6 min.; remove from oven and allow to stand 5 min. before removing from baking sheet. *Makes about 4 doz. cookies.*

Note: *Do not use self-rising flour in this recipe.*

LACE ROLL-UPS

See color picture, p. 119.

Make French Lace Cookies (left)—except while they are still warm, roll into a cylindrical shape. There is a magic moment when Lace Cookies are cool enough to roll yet not so cool that they will break in rolling. Keep trying until you find that moment. If cookies do cool too much, return to the oven for a minute.

PEEK-A-BOWS

Make Lace Roll-ups (above). When cool, tie with gaily colored ribbon.

Historical Highlights

1962—Colonel John Glenn orbited the earth in a rocket-boosted space ship.

1968—Apollo 8 orbited the moon.

1969—Apollo 11's Neil Armstrong became the first man to set foot on the moon.

EASY CREAMY ICING

1 cup sifted confec-
    tioners' sugar
¼ tsp. salt

½ tsp. vanilla or
    other flavoring
1½ tbsp. cream or
    1 tbsp. water

Blend sugar, salt, and flavoring (try lemon, almond, or peppermint flavoring for variety). Add cream to make easy to spread. If desired, tint with a few drops of food coloring. Spread on cookies with spatula or pastry brush. *Makes icing for 3 to 5 doz. cookies, depending on size.*

HINT

For professional looking iced drop cookies, place 1 tsp. icing on center of each cooky. With small icing spatula, spread icing with circular motion.

MARIE'S CHOCOLATE ICING

1 tbsp. butter
1 sq. unsweetened
    chocolate (1 oz.)

1½ tbsp. warm water
1 cup sifted confec-
    tioners' sugar

Melt butter and chocolate over hot water. Blend in warm water. Beat in confectioners' sugar until icing spreads easily. *Makes icing to frost 9" sq. pan of cookies or 3 to 4 doz. cookies.*

BUTTER ICING

2½ tbsp. soft butter
1½ cups sifted con-
    fectioners' sugar

1½ tbsp. cream
¾ tsp. vanilla

Blend butter and sugar together. Stir in cream and vanilla until smooth. *Makes icing for 4 doz. cookies.*

BROWNED BUTTER ICING

Make Butter Icing (above)—except brown butter in saucepan over medium heat until a delicate brown. Blend with sugar.

ORANGE BUTTER ICING

Make Butter Icing (above)—except use 1½ tbsp. orange juice and 2 tsp. grated orange rind in place of cream and vanilla.

LEMON BUTTER ICING

Make Butter Icing (above)—except use 1½ tbsp lemon juice and 2 tsp. grated lemon rind in place of cream and vanilla.

MOCHA BUTTER ICING

Make Butter Icing (above)—except omit cream and vanilla and blend in 1 tsp. powdered instant coffee dissolved in 1 tbsp. hot water. If icing is too thick to spread, add a few drops of water.

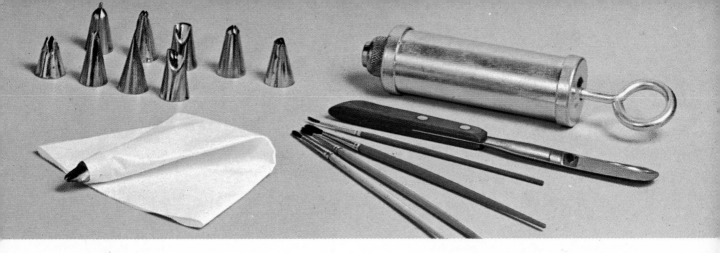

QUICK CREAM ICING

Blend 1½ cups sifted confectioners' sugar, ¼ tsp. vanilla, and enough cream (2 to 3 tbsp.) to make a thin icing. *Makes icing for 15x10″ pan of cookies.*

DECORATOR ICING

Combine 1½ to 2 cups sifted confectioners' sugar with 1 to 2 tbsp. water (just enough to make icing easy to force through decorating tube yet hold its shape).

BROWNED BUTTER GLAZE

¼ cup butter
1 cup sifted confec-
tioners' sugar

½ tsp. vanilla
1 to 2 tbsp. hot water

Melt butter until golden brown. Blend in sugar and vanilla. Stir in hot water until icing spreads smoothly. *Makes icing for about 30 cookies.*

THIN CONFECTIONERS' SUGAR ICING

Mix 1 cup sifted confectioners' sugar; 1 to 2 tbsp. milk, water, or cream; and ½ tsp. vanilla until smooth.

PEANUT BUTTER ICING

Delicious on Chocolate Slices (p. 16).

2 tbsp. chunk-style
peanut butter
2 to 3 tbsp. milk

1½ cups sifted
confectioners'
sugar

Stir all ingredients together until creamy.

FROSTING "CEMENT"

For our charming Cooky House (pp. 64-65).

2 egg whites
½ tsp. cream of tartar

2 cups sifted confec-
tioners' sugar
food coloring

Using electric mixer, beat egg whites with cream of tartar until stiff. Gradually beat in 1 cup of sugar. Beat 10 min. Beat in second cup of sugar; beat 10 min. more. During last few minutes of beating, add food coloring for desired color. While using or storing the frosting "cement," press transparent plastic wrap directly on top of frosting in bowl to prevent drying; lift wrap just long enough to remove "cement" for each application.

THIN CHOCOLATE ICING

1 sq. unsweetened
chocolate (1 oz.)
1 tsp. butter

1 cup sifted confec-
tioners' sugar
2 tbsp. boiling water

Melt chocolate and butter together over hot water. Remove from heat. Blend in sugar and water. Beat only until smooth but not stiff.

OUT OF CHOCOLATE?

If you run out of chocolate, use cocoa. Substitute 3 tbsp. cocoa plus 1 tbsp. butter or margarine for 1 sq. unsweetened chocolate.

❧ INDEX ❧